The Smart Approach to
COUNTRY
DECORATING

WITHDRAWN

CRE▲TIVE
HOMEOWNER®

The Smart Approach to
COUNTRY
DECORATING

Margaret Sabo Wills

CREATIVE HOMEOWNER®, Upper Saddle River, New Jersey

Publisher: Natalie Chapman

Editorial Director: Timothy O. Bakke
Creative Director: Clarke Barre
Art Director: Monduane Harris
Production Manager: Kimberly H. Vivas

Senior Editor, Home Decorating: Kathie Robitz
Photo Editor: Stanley F. Sudol

Senior Designer: Glee Barre
Illustrator: Robert LaPointe

Copy Editor: Ellie Sweeney
Glossary Compilation: Sharon Ranftle
Proofreaders: Sharon Ranftle, Dan Houghtaling
Indexer: Schroeder Indexing Services

Cover Design: Clarke Barre
Cover Photography: Jessie Walker Associates
Back Cover Photography: *right* Brad Simmons; *top and bottom left* Jessie Walker Associates

Current Printing (last digit)
10 9 8 7 6 5 4 3 2 1

The Smart Approach to Country Decorating, First Edition
Library of Congress Catalog Card Number:2001090767
ISBN: 1-58011-081-9

CREATIVE HOMEOWNER®
A Division of Federal Marketing Corp.
24 Park Way
Upper Saddle River, NJ 07458
Web site: **www.creativehomeowner.com**

DEDICATION

For my family—
The one I came from,
The one I joined up with,
The one I've made with Rosalind and Benedict, who give true meaning to
"pride and joy," and my husband, Stewart, my dearest love, who makes me
laugh, broadens my mind, and gives me strength.

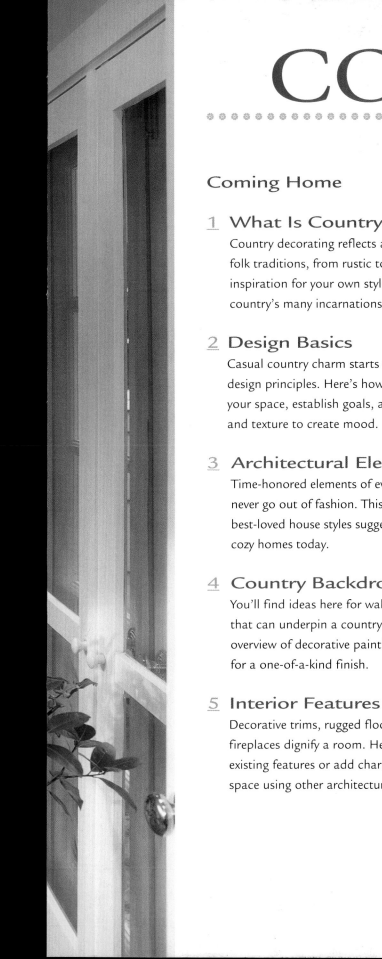

CONTENTS

COMING HOME
To Country

ountry as a decorating term can be defined only loosely—and that's fine with most country-decorating enthusiasts. They're drawn to a style that offers the comfort of the familiar and traditional yet allows plenty of scope for the highly individual imagination.

Country rooms are easygoing and seldom confined to a specific historical period. They hark back to a time when people lived closer to the land and in tune with nature, when life was harder but less frenetic than it is today.

In earlier times, objects were made for a specific purpose—homeowners who needed a chair or a shelf or a

basket either asked a local artisan to produce one or made it themselves. Conversely, today's manufacturers determine our "needs" and produce identical goods in mass quantities. While our industrial age tempts us to buy copious material products, country decorating encourages us to pare down to fewer but more-treasured things.

Despite appreciating our modern technology and conveniences, we may need to hold on to simpler pleasures. It's natural to romanticize the past, and amid the accelerating social changes of the nineteenth century, the United States' 1876 centennial celebration prompted a nostalgic "Colonial Revival" in decorating. In the Jazz Age of the 1920s, Tudor and Georgian houses filled the booming new suburbs. Closer to our own time, following the 1976 bicentennial and the tumult of the preceding decade, America rediscovered its heritage of painted furniture, rag rugs, tole ware, and quilts.

Putting aside the ebb-and-flow of fashion, we keep returning to country decorating because it restores our surroundings to a human scale and celebrates the charm in everyday things. The country room's decorative flourishes incline toward rustic baskets, pottery jugs, whittled and carved woods, colorful needlework, or casual displays of collections gathered over the years. It's rich with objects that show the work of hands or reflect personal stories. And to add a touch of spice, there are accessories and collectibles that sum up country spirit, especially when we display them to advantage.

This book lays the groundwork for country surroundings by reviewing interior design fundamentals—texture, scale, pattern, and color—and how they can create country flavor. We'll also look at the exterior and interior architectural details. To fill these evocative spaces, we'll survey a wide menu of timeless fabrics, finishes, and furniture. We'll endeavor to help you realize the potential of your personal country aesthetic. Throughout the book, we'll touch lightly on history. We can't

live in any time but the present, however, and country decorating is not about dreamy nostalgia. It's about creating rooms that are practical, fun, and personal—rooms that you can enjoy today but that lend a little old-fashioned charm to the daily routine. Country decorating also adds a distinction and a considerably welcoming mood to almost any type of architecture. All it takes is an imaginative spirit and your ability to trust your own personal likes and tastes. After all, country decorating cannot be defined by any one personality but by diversity. 🐝

Patterns and texture are the base upon which a successful and welcoming country motif is established, opposite.

Country decorating lends itself to a relaxed type of living. Food, festive crockery, and fresh-cut flowers all contribute to the overall country aesthetic, below.

1

WHAT IS COUNTRY?
Defining the Look

If you're reading this book, you've probably already developed some answers to the chapter's opening question. Country style draws on history and a sense of connection with those who came before us. It emphasizes the homegrown and the handmade. In this view, a room is never "done"—it evolves over time. Our ancestors didn't discard things as new styles came along, but turned items to new uses. Often, we love homey objects because they show such ingenuity. When we freely mix objects from different eras, our rooms have a relaxed, eclectic, and high-spirited look.

Eclectic Appeal

the true essence of country decorating comes from a unique ability to mix and match a wide variety of styles, objects, and ideas. A well-developed country room speaks of years of acquiring and preserving momentos, treasured furniture, and beloved pieces of art. A home that is brought together through thought and attention to detail speaks volumes compared with one that is assembled, prepackaged, and purchased as a set. People who crave complete comfort in their home will strive to fill it with those things that bring beauty, personality, and convenience into their everyday lives.

For those with an adventurous spirit and a strong sense of likes and dislikes, an eclectic space comes together with little fuss or consternation. However, if you fear that a Georgian mirror looks out of place over a primitive side table, a mix-and-match approach may not be compatible with your sensibilities. But if you're willing to take a few decorating chances, start slowly.

* Begin by mingling pieces of similar subjects, but of different sizes, periods, and colors.
* Experiment with various furniture arrangements. Angle pieces and move them away from walls.
* Brave momentary shock and allow the look to grow on you.

Traditionally, the appearance of a country room is simply a working background for a busy life. Beauty is often a byproduct of the textures and colors of honest necessities—the weathered wood of a much-scrubbed table, the soft wool of a lap robe, and the rough stone of a fireplace surround. Yet our ancestors didn't hesitate to embellish the necessities. Where a plain piece would serve just as well, they'd weave a bright pattern into a basket, carve the handles of wooden ware, stencil a floor, or decorate the furniture with freehand painting.

COUNTRY'S MANY FACETS

This book will incline toward America's country traditions from the seventeenth to the early twentieth century. But American Country is an especially broad river, fed by many meandering streams. In your decorating reveries, you may feel drawn toward one of those tributaries. The varied approaches to country decorating do not fall into strict categories. They do, however, borrow from many cultures.

INTERNATIONAL APPEAL

Folk traditions around the world share many basic elements—the rugged woods, the natural colors, the satisfying solidity of stone, clay, and plaster, and the natural fibers. The details provide local flavor. Here's a survey of some of country's many international interpretations.

English Country Style. Even as the American colonies rebelled against British rule, they still followed Britain's decorative lead. English Country offers two disparate inspirations: the grand manor and the humble cottage. To suggest the country manor house in your own decorating efforts, imagine an aristocratic household, over generations, filling the large rooms of a family estate with heirlooms and the occasional skillfully crafted new piece. Grand, lushly draped windows should complement the substantial furniture and overstuffed upholstery, which, depending on the season, could sport worn leather or casual linen slipcovers. And carved furnishings of fine oak and mahogany might include some slightly worn pieces retired from "city dwellings." In an English Country house, the fabrics tend toward fine, if somewhat aged, chintzes, wools, and linens rather than sophisticated satins and velvets. The clutter should appear comfortable and personal, with family portraits, books, photos, souvenirs, and maybe an Oriental rug or two. Tiled

Diverse traditions in a modest space, above, with French Country yellow-ochre walls and floral chintzes play off a New England sea chest and an early nineteenth-century American portrait.

fireplaces or papered walls can add another layer of pattern and print to a room.

The humbler English Cottage look is charmingly cluttered, although with more rustic touches. There may be rough-finished plaster walls with sturdy exposed beams or a planked chair rail. The woods tend toward "deal," the British term for fir or pine, which was often painted and sometimes stenciled in centuries past. Stone, tile, or wood are typically underfoot, and homespun gingham and stripes often frame small windows. Useful baskets, throws, rugs, and candles may commonly double as decorative accents.

Swedish Country Style. In the late eighteenth century, King Gustav III of Sweden and the Swedish aristocracy embraced the formal neoclassicism of France and England. This enthusiasm filtered down to Sweden's provinces, which, in turn, created symmetrical rooms designed around a palette of buttercream yellow, gentle blue, and dove gray. To re-create the look, think of bleached floors, gilded mirrors, and large bare or lightly dressed windows (originally intended to maximize Sweden's sunlight). Light woods—birch and alder for formal rooms and pine and beech for humbler spaces—often feature carving.

These so-called Gustavian touches blend with the earthier Swedish traditional handcrafts of painted furniture, stenciled and faux-marbled architectural trim, and striped rag rugs and runners tinted with natural dyes. Kitchens, which originally provided a special focus, can be brightened with yellow ware pottery and copper pots or pudding molds.

French Country Style. To suggest French Country ambiance, recall the warm climate of the southern Provence region and the brilliant sunshine that entranced nineteenth-century British travelers. Here the classic farmhouse, like dwellings in many hot regions, fends off the midday heat with massive stone and clay walls that may wear washes of gold, rosy pink, or cool blue-violet tints. Local terra-cotta tile floors, with fancy hand-painted glazed tiles, brighten the interior.

Mediterranean trade, which introduced exotic fabrics from Asia, spurred France's textile industry. You can evoke a French Provincial mood by using bright cottons in small-scale prints, especially those with designs in saturated blues, yellows, and reds that glow in the sunlight.

In keeping with France's love of good food, the kitchen boasts bright pottery

An arched window, opposite, set into massive masonry walls, summons up the solidity of a generations-old country villa. Pots of fragrant herbs and fine copper cookware on the wide work counters complete a picture of quaint sophistication.

and copperwares. Influenced by the aristocracy's ornate furniture, farmhouse chairs and tables feature gentle curves and simple carvings. You could emphasize a few solid pieces, such as an armoire filled with table linens and china.

Italian Country Style. Like Provence, rural Italy is scattered with villas and farmhouses boasting large, breeze-swept rooms of thick masonry that open onto wide courtyards and shadowy verandas. To create an Italian flavor, paint plastered walls with soft, faded colors such as earthy tints of red and yellow ochre, and use russet terra-cotta tile or quarried stone for the floors. Try fabrics that are rich but simple, with stripes or woven textures. Install shutters on windows to imitate Italian Country's similar window attire.

For a quaint kitchen cor-ner with a retro flavor, right, an old-fashioned table and chairs were given a distressed paint finish. A circa 1940s cotton cloth, vintage stove, and linoleum floor pull the look together.

The colors of the walls and textiles on display in this family room, oppo-site, were inspired by southern Europe's natural hues and textures.

In Tuscany, the abundant wood supply encouraged elegantly carved furniture finished with buffed wax, a soft color-wash, or bold hand-painted flourishes. Furniture here tends to be arranged symmetrically, against the walls, with a formal spareness. Bright tiles and pottery recall the region's colorful ambiance.

COMPATIBLE STYLES AND INFLUENCES

Unless you are a purist, you can mix other styles with most country decors. Some styles are more compatible than others. If you like an eclectic approach to pulling together a look for your country-style home, consider one of the following.

Shaker. Shaker craftsmen reduced the era's familiar country furniture—the slat-back chair, the rocker, the candle stand—to graceful, sturdy essentials. The quest for plain and practical surroundings, free of distracting ornament, created a fertile source of design inspiration and furniture of beautiful austerity.

Shaker rooms are spare. The usually whitewashed walls can be set off by simple chair rails, built-in cabinetry, and often an upper peg rail where chairs or baskets can be hung out of the way. Chair seats are often webbed with red or blue fabric tape, while woodwork can be painted in rich blues, grays, and greens. Today, many manufacturers offer Shaker-inspired furniture and accessories.

Victorian. The high-spirited nineteenth century offered a grab bag of design ideals. Victorian decorating summons images of high-style rooms lavish with rich colors, abundant ornament, and pattern-on-pattern fabric and wallcovering. Original Victorian interiors were dark, and heavy draperies diluted the light over convoluted button-tufted fringed furniture. Today's rendition of the look is lighter and less cluttered. Victorian Country is a charming cottage style—relaxed, slightly whimsical, and informal—with airy window treatments, gingerbread trim, and wicker furniture.

Arts and Crafts. Arts and Crafts glorifies hand craftsmanship and natural materials. Furniture pieces demand a rich wood background with paneling, squared pillars, and heavily framed doorways. Other accoutrements may include a stone fireplace, hand-molded tile, hammered-copper trimmings, stained glass, and fabrics and wallcoverings with stylized floral and geometric patterns.

Western Styles. Picture the rugged ranch houses of the American West with their rough wood walls, plank floors, pinched-tin chests, and wide windows dressed in

Straight-back rockers with webbed seats, left, rest in a screened porch amid a profusion of rugged baskets and farmhouse necessities. Homey everyday pieces such as these were further simplified to their essential forms by nineteenth-century Shaker craftsmen.

The Western version of country, opposite, may incorporate Spanish influences, as demonsrated by the primitive-style furniture and bold colors and patterns in this bedroom.

gingham and calico. Or evoke the region's Spanish heritage with smooth adobe walls and carved furniture draped in woven wools of natural white or vivid blues and Cochineal Red. A literal interpretation of the style would also include vivid Native American textiles and other craft pieces.

Retro Country. Vintage 1930s and '40s kitchen linens in primary-color prints of flowers, teacups, and puppies are at home with the era's bright pottery and streamlined housewares. The furniture, slightly pared down or covered in contrasting veneers, stops short of the urban Art Deco look. ✖

What Is Country? 21

2
DESIGN BASICS
With Country in Mind

Aiming for country charm doesn't mean that you can shortcut any steps in the interior design process. A room that appears to be a delightful happenstance usually springs from methodical planning. One hurdle, never imagined by our ancestors, is today's vast array of choices. While a few lucky homeowners can forge ahead sure of their instincts about the right color and mix of patterns and prints, most of us quail before the rows of wallpaper books, fabric swatches, and paint chips, and hesitate to start the interlocked chain of decisions. Sometimes too much can be impossible to handle, especially when you're on a budget.

The room's advantages deserve the focus. The fireplace, below, gains importance and seems even cozier with a worn leather chair and old chest angled alongside.

smart steps

A PLAN OF ACTION

A well-planned room not only pleases the eye but comfortably meets your practical needs. Before you make time-consuming and sometimes costly mistakes, take the time to analyze the project. What do you want to achieve? What's realistic given all the circumstances and factors? Here are a few big-picture planning steps that can suggest routes through the thickets.

one **Know yourself and your needs.** Picture in detail how you and your family will use the room and how that drives your design agenda. To gear a room for reading or working on crafts, keep an eye out for country-friendly task lighting—maybe a handsome brass floor lamp or a vintage gooseneck fixture. For watching TV, choose comfortable, country-style seating. A high-traffic entry might argue for easily maintained sealed quarry tiles instead of pastel carpeting. But for a busy family space, you might prefer a patterned rug that camouflages dirt and muffles the din.

two **Know your space.** Good design begins with a careful analysis of the space, even if you have the leeway to make structural changes. Begin with the positives. What do you like best about the room? What makes it special? What's the first thing you see when you enter? If the room lacks a natural focal point, consider what piece of furniture or artwork, possibly relocated from another room, could step into that role. On the flip side, determine the flaws to be played down.

three **Take the time to troubleshoot.** Seek decorative solutions for day-to-day annoyances. Is the couch a catchall for papers and books? Set big baskets or a pretty hand-painted box nearby to stow the clutter. If the entry presents a mess of boots and coats, a rack topped with an old-fashioned mitten box can sort it out.

four **Clarify the scope of your project.** Will redecorating require a major overhaul with a string of purchases or just some strategic sprucing-up with touches of country flavor? Take stock of your resources, and determine your budget. What do you already have that, in fine country tradition, can be refurbished or used in a new way? Also consider your intended project's timeframe.

While its rich woodwork and brick background evoke an 1800s farmhouse, this country kitchen, above, includes ample workspaces and user-friendly storage.

ORGANIZING

Country decorating can tempt us
with too many possibilities.
Keep them straight with a design
notebook of samples, swatches,
brochures, sketches,
torn-out magazine pages, and
notes to yourself. When the raw
materials are all in one place,
you may see connections, garner fresh
ideas, and be able to
discuss plans with family
members or salespeople
more clearly.

PLANNING A ROOM'S PURPOSE

The interiors of the oldest homes tended toward large, all-purpose "great halls." But houses of the nineteenth and early twentieth centuries often contained a series of separate rooms. A prosperous Victorian household might have a company parlor and a family parlor, a music room, a casual morning room for the lady of the house, and even a smoking room. With a compartmentalized floor plan, you might want to play up the coziness and privacy of each space while using related colors or the same flooring throughout to visually connect them. Coordinating fabrics and related furniture styles provide other links.

Since the mid-twentieth century, floor plans have returned to open, multipurpose interiors. Clever decorating touches can signal the separate functions of adjoining spaces such as a dining corner and the work area. One drawback to an open floor plan is the need to keep things clean and provide ample storage because everything is in view. For a multipurpose room, hunt for country-style storage solutions—plain chests ripe for decorative painting, big rough baskets, or a slim shelf to fill an otherwise useless corner.

To explore the possibilities of a given space, draw the room on paper. Measure the room carefully, noting architectural features such as fireplaces, windows, and doors, including each door-swing space. Then create a scaled floor plan on graph paper, and draw scaled furniture templates of existing pieces and intended purchases. With these tools, you can experiment with different working arrangements before moving furniture.

Try to look at a familiar space with fresh eyes. Automatically arranging furniture against the walls can give a space the personality of a waiting room. Bring furnishings away from the walls, or place them at an angle to make the room more inviting. Arrange intimate groupings to facilitate conversation and deflect cross-traffic. Clustering seating pieces may also open up space for a quiet desk corner or a reading chair away from the action.

STRIKING AN ATTITUDE

Before decorating a room, consider what "attitude" it will have. Knowing this will help you to organize your project plans. As noted in the previous chapter, country decorating can be earthy and serene, detailed and dignified, or bright and whim-

The airy, rounded forms of wicker, bent wood, and twining ivy harmonize into a contemplative desk corner, above, a little apart from a busy house.

A carefully-wrought theme of soft colors and simple forms, opposite right, gives a bedroom under the eaves a restful attitude.

Decoratively stash clutter away with country storage pieces, opposite left, such as a stack of painted boxes.

Repeated motifs add up to a calm coherence. In a Shaker-simple dining room, square-lined furniture, trimmed in lively checks, is echoed by square-framed artworks in neat rows.

sical. Elements from different eras or ethnic backgrounds can come together if they are equally formal or rustic and share a similar spirit. When shopping for furniture and accessories, keep the room's tone in mind. While it's fine to add an occasional bracing dash of contrast, not all impulse purchases will look natural in a given room, even if they're beautiful on their own.

A room's attitude arises from its colors, forms, and textures. These abstract concepts, while inextricably mixed in the real-life room, can be considered separately in the planning. Color has such power that it's covered separately in Chapter 8, "The Colors of Country," beginning on page 130.

A MATTER OF FORM

Although you'll find shapes and lines of infinite variety, each group has its own decorative connotations.

Straight lines underpin the art of home building and impart a reassuring sense of solidity and regularity. They fit together efficiently, as demonstrated by a bank of bookcases. Used vertically, straight lines make a room seem grand and formal—picture English country manors and Victorian row houses with towering ceilings.

Long, low horizontal lines are more restful and intimate, suggesting a cottage-like ambiance. Grouping objects or furniture of similar heights, or aligning a wallpaper border with doorway headers, for example, fosters harmonious horizontal lines.

Curved lines tend to be romantic and lush—think of a wraparound staircase, curvaceous chairs, exotic arched doorways, and friendly round tables.

FOOL
THE EYE

remember

that it's not the actual size of the room, it's how large or small it feels.

To make space feel larger:

- Unify it with flowing, repetitive patterns, full-length window treatments, and colors that blend together. Avoid sharp contrasts.
- Stress light, cool colors or pale neutrals.
- Limit furniture to the essentials, and leave open spaces to rest the eye.
- Expose floor space with leggy furniture.

To make space feel cozier:

- Partition the room with dividers, screens, and storage pieces, or extend it visually with pools of light, area rugs, and different wall colors.
- Vary the heights of furnishings, and group pieces into functional areas.
- Fill the space with bold patterns and large-scale furniture styled to sit solidly on the floor.
- Consider warm, dark colors and matte textures that absorb light and soften sound for privacy.

Painted furniture, sisal rugs, and white-washed walls, left, create a light, neutral background to visually open up a sunny bedroom.

Clustering the furniture around a canopy-draped bed, below, gives this room a cozy yet airy ambiance thanks to the soft colors and fabrics.

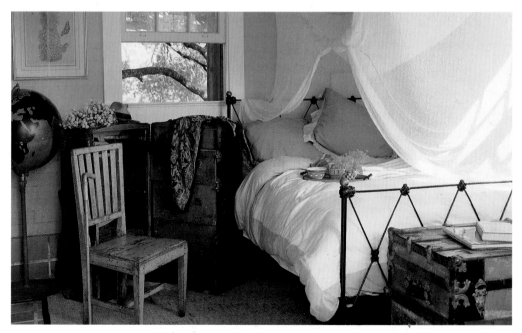

Flowerpots of sunny yellow wildflowers, covered in rough twigs and twine, opposite, combine natural elements—one of country decorating's enduring themes.

The timeless texture of wood, natural or roughly painted, below, unifies a foyer's casual grouping of handcrafted pieces.

Angles, because they're relatively uncommon in houses, tend to be dynamic and eye-catching, as in lively dormered windows or the bold diagonal line of an open stairway. Diagonal lines in any form suggest change or movement.

TEXTURAL PLAYS

Texture, whether visual or tactile, creates sensual appeal. Everyone experiences a room differently when walking on carpet versus flagstone, or sitting on velvet cushions versus those of cotton duck. Flocked wallpaper is more tactile than painted eggshell satin walls. Some textures, such as a sponge-painted finish, merely lend the illusion of depth. Adding texture will enliven a room of subdued colors.

Smooth, shiny surfaces make colors appear lighter and brilliant—picture the difference between pillows in gray satin and gray wool. High-gloss finishes tend to have a sophisticated, manufactured feeling, which in excess could undermine the warm earthiness of a country room. Used sparingly, however, glossy accents such as a polished pair of candlesticks or the sheen of new chintz can give rugged homespuns and matte woods a welcome lift.

Rough textures blur colors and give objects visual weight and solidity. Textured walls seem to draw inward for a cozier, enclosed feeling. Truly rugged textures, such as brick or barn siding, create a play of light and shadows. On the practical side, shiny surfaces are easier to clean, but they tend to show every speck and smudge. Matte finishes give dirt a better foothold but more readily forgive daily use as they camouflage some spots or fingerprints.

Determining a room's purpose and personality will serve as your decorating road map, but your plans should allow for a few spontaneous detours. After all, the fun of country decorating is in finding an old weathered armoire with hand painting or falling in love with a fabric that's bolder than any design or color you ever pictured in your home. The aim of country decorating isn't to achieve the impersonal prettiness of a showcase room but to create an expressive space that responds to people's changing interests and tastes. 🐚

3

ARCHITECTURAL ELEMENTS
Of Country

I n the newest subdivision skirting your town, you'll likely see houses sporting all manner of old-fashioned details—columns, pediments, porches, divided-light windows, and dormers. These time-honored elements of everyday architecture have never gone out of style. Learning about the houses of the past can suggest ways to capture their grace in our homes today. Architects who were well versed in the latest vogue designed many of the past's urban residences and commercial buildings, and it's easy to see where these buildings fit in design history. Country houses, however, tend to be idiosyncratic.

Traditional details often grace modern buildings. Multilight windows, left, harking back to an era when even small panes of glass were costly, are ganged together here for a sun-drenched stairwell.

A fireplace, opposite, with a full-height wall of multitoned brick, is the warm focus of this country house.

These less prestigious structures often embodied the handiwork of local craftsmen. Although they generally hesitated to adopt new styles, many country craftsmen incorporated a few of the fancier details that could be found in the architecture of the cities or towns. Some of these elements persisted in country homes and furnishings long after their city heyday. And when new generations craved more space, thrifty homebuilders simply tacked on additions without paying mind to a dwelling's original architectural "style." Because these uninhibited, less classically trained country builders cheerfully grafted new design elements onto older structures, many country houses defy categorization.

AN AMERICAN HOUSE TOUR

America's earliest settlers focused on survival rather than style and used the abundant wood from cleared farmland to fashion house beams and pegged timbers. The dwellings of many of New England's first settlements resembled England's post-and-beam farmers' single-room cottages.

In 1638, Swedish colonists in the Delaware River valley built America's first log cabins. Stacked rough logs chinked with moss and clay framed out each rectangular structure, which sometimes boasted two rooms and a loft. Stripping the bark and porous sapwood to use only the log's more durable heartwood (called "squaring off") was more laborious, but it helped settlers stack the logs smoothly. One strong person with a heavy ax and a hunting knife could build a log cabin, and a group of settlers could quickly raise a small community. Until the westward pioneers reached the tree-poor prairies, the log cabin remained a standard type of frontier dwelling. Country decorating at its most rustic evokes the characteristics of these earliest, simple houses—full of earthy textures and natural hues.

THE QUEST FOR COMFORT

The single room soon became two rooms, then four, clustered around a central chimney. When times were good, a farmer constructed a dormered half-story, creating the Cape Cod–style house. Or he might build a full second story under an A-framed, gable roof.

A two-story structure with a one-story lean-to under a long sloping roof fashioned what New Englanders called a saltbox for its resemblance to a wall-hung kitchen storage box. In the traditional Colonial farmhouse, a central staircase hall divided the front parlors and led to a long "keeping room" at the rear that contained the cooking fireplace.

During the early 1700s, the front facade became symmetrical. Houses featured paneled doors and heavy iron hardware. Larger nine- or twelve-pane double-hung windows supplanted earlier tiny casement versions. Britain's dignified neoclassic styles, loosely designated as Georgian, influenced these American Colonial houses.

Weathered gray shingles and the long, asymmetrical roofline, above, typify a timeless New England saltbox house.

Squared logs, white-washed on the interior side, right, form an earthy, appealing background to a summer-home kitchen.

Elaborate moldings and
ornament, opposite,
dress up this elegant
wraparound porch on a
handsome old Queen
Anne–style Victorian
house.

A simple farmhouse
porch, below, links the
original structure to an
addition.

A SENSE OF PLACE

While British influence predominated, America's early homes also displayed a delightful variety of elements reflecting the occupants' ethnic origins, local materials, and the climate. Northerners built compact homes centered with a chimney. Because of the New England climate, people sometimes linked their farmhouses to barns in order to reach their livestock during even the worst blizzards. Southerners, by contrast, located fireplaces on end walls to dissipate the heat or placed the kitchen in a separate structure that they reached through a breezeway. Many southern styles raised the house on a high basement foundation or on

SMART TIP

PORCHES

Around the world, people love outdoor spaces—courtyards, porches, balconies, verandas, and even the few steps of a front stoop. If you're thinking of adding or enlarging a country porch, here are a few considerations. How will the porch suit the house's design, spirit, and scale? A Victorian porch in full gingerbread might look awkward on a streamlined split-level.

How will the addition affect the interior's natural light and traffic patterns?

Do zoning regulations dictate a porch's placement, size, and materials?

What about safety, especially with a raised porch? Painted wood can be slippery when wet. Be sure steps and floors are properly sloped to drain water.

Have you tailored the porch plan to its intended uses and climate? A screened porch would be welcome on a mosquito-prone waterside home.

An angled gambrel roof, left, suggests a German or Dutch influence in many old American houses and their modern descendants.

open, stacked-stone piers in order to catch the breezes.

Dutch and German settlers in the Hudson River valley, New Jersey, and Pennsylvania favored native fieldstone or quarried materials. They typically fashioned a long, rectangular structure with two front entrances. Along the Hudson River valley, a classic gambrel roof characteristic of the Dutch Colonial style often topped the stone houses.

In the southern or middle colonies, French design influences often prompted a sloped-in, or hipped, roofline, which gave the house a less massive look. Along the French-influenced Mississippi River valley, the long, steep-sloped hip roof usually descended to a wraparound porch.

In the Southwest, Spanish influences combined with Native American building traditions encouraged adobe mud-brick buildings. This basic one-room structure soon evolved into a series of linked spaces surrounding a courtyard.

A YOUNG, GROWING NATION

From the 1790s to the 1830s, fashionable tastes adopted the delicately scaled neoclassicism of the Federal style, which was inspired by Georgian design.

Though related to robust Georgian houses, Federal houses tended toward slimmer columns, less-ornate windows and doorways, and sleeker ornamentation featuring shallow carved panels and swags. Although mostly decorative, graceful oval or round windows also proved popular at the time.

Early nineteenth-century America, perhaps noting a parallel with its own democracy, admired the art and architecture of classical Greece. This enthusiasm prompted what was then called the National style, which we now designate as the Greek Revival style. This architecture evokes a Greek temple's design. On these buildings, you'll see triangular pediments atop fluted columns or pilasters that frame wide porches or porticos. Architectural details include Hellenistic reeding; dentil and egg-and-dart moldings; fanlights over windows and doors; and carved festoons, urns, and acanthus leaves.

America's nineteenth-century Greek Revival style, below, evokes a Grecian temple with triangular pediments, pilasters, columns, and long windows.

Light, tall, and dignified also describes the effect of Greek Revival architecture. While showcased in grand antebellum plantation houses and in major public monuments, this style enlivened many country homes built between 1820 and 1860. Many a modest farmhouse hinted at Greek Revival aspirations only with its gabled front, long windows, and simple pilasters alongside the door.

Pockets of ethnic building influences—such as the German half-timbered houses in Texas and the brightly painted Scandinavian-inspired structures that populated the Upper Midwest—retained a presence in America's architectural vocabulary. But regional differences were succumbing to the widely distributed "pattern books" that promoted the most recent styles of the day.

EXPANDING POSSIBILITIES

Because of the nineteenth century's rapid industrialization and new transportation networks, builders were able to work with mass-produced brick, quarried stone, glass, and prefabricated trim and moldings. Heavy post-and-beam joinery gave way to "balloon" framing, once a derisive term for the now-familiar stud-and-platform construction that used thinner, standardized lumber. Such streamlined building methods helped to create new towns on

A library, above, that freely mixes country and modern hints at the Victorian fondness for angles and eccentric window shapes.

Lively windows, with latticework and curved shapes, opposite, invigorate an exterior that harks back to high-spirited Victorian homes.

the frontier and new suburbs around older cities. During this unsettling period, homeowners took comfort in a variety of revival styles combined with the latest conveniences and technologies.

One enduring nineteenth-century architectural revival, called Gothic style, takes license with the medieval era's cathedrals, encouraging complex and asymmetrical forms. While the wealthy generally chose multicolor stone or multitone brick to clad their homes, Carpenter Gothic country cottages and farmhouses rendered the style in wood. These houses displayed vertical board-and-batten

siding to underscore height, strong rooflines, and large porches traced with gingerbread trimmings and brackets created with the newly invented scroll saw.

The era's Italianate houses showcased horizontal lines with rows of round-arched windows, towers, and often a mansard roof with a flat top and steeply sloped sides. Instead of lively gingerbread, the roof's deep overhang rested on heavy carved brackets. Builders created smooth stucco surfaces and sometimes scored them to mimic the look of stone block. Alternatively, they used wood painted in muted, stonelike colors. An arched colonnade fronted the large, Italianate porches.

The 1876 centennial celebration reawakened popular interest in early America. Victorian Queen Anne houses boasted Colonial details such as divided-light windows, door pediments, scroll-work, lattice, and decorative "fish-scale" and diamond shingles. These houses freely mixed finishing materials and emphasized angles with projecting bays,

A wraparound porch with lacy gingerbread architectural trim looks as inviting now as such spaces did in the past.

deep niches, and towers. The newly available premixed paints made it easier to coordinate a multihued polychrome exterior. Queen Anne architecture bore similarities to the Stick style, which showcased the home's bones with decora-

Two Classic Building Methods Revisited

log cabins have changed in our time from rough, temporary shelters or casual, seasonal retreats into high-vaulted, multilevel, year-round homes with every modern convenience. The chinking has been replaced with advanced tongue-and-groove joinery, modern sealants, and flexible gaskets that accommodate settling and prevent air infiltration. Logs milled to different profiles can now emulate exterior clapboard siding, too.

post-and-beam

construction, used for centuries to build cozy cottages and high-lofted barns, has experienced a modern resurgence. It uses the outside walls framed in mortise-and-tenon-joined lumber to carry the weight of the structure and relegates the interior walls to mere partitions. This construction method creates soaring, open spaces that are sleek and sunlit. The post-and-beam framework can be filled with prefabricated panels of modern, energy-efficient materials or with standard studs covered with drywall. While traditional siding usually sheathes the exteriors, interiors often expose and display their handsome wood "bones."

HISTORIC DISTRICTS

If your love of old houses leads you to consider moving to a designated historic district, consider the facts. Before purchasing a historic house, check how much authority the local historical society and architectural review boards have, and determine their efficiency in handing out the necessary approvals. Sometimes even the color you choose to paint the exterior of the house must be approved by the board. Know what restrictions and compliances you must adhere to before you buy.

tive cross braces, visible framing members, and straight braces beneath porch overhangs. Conversely, the Shingle style, popular in resort areas, highlighted the house's "skin," using textured shingles painted in deep red, gray, brown, olive green, or yellow ocher to cover the rambling turrets and wide porches.

The beloved Midwestern farmhouses of the late 1800s often embodied, in understated form, Victorian flourishes borrowed from their city cousins. Porches were often adorned with spindle posts, brackets, gingerbread, gables, and dormers. White finishes remained popular in rural areas, though more fashionable polychrome exteriors also prevailed.

SIMPLER FORMS

By the late nineteenth century, the reaction against ornate Victoriana had already gathered steam. England's Arts and Crafts design movement stressed the individuality and beauty of handcrafted natural materials and promoted strong, clear forms and flat patterning. In America, this movement inspired a variety of modest houses.

During the early part of the twentieth century, Frank Lloyd Wright, one of America's most innovative architects, promoted his organic Prairie-style houses. These homes emphasized open, sunlit interiors, mellow natural hues, and horizontal lines that integrated the house with its natural surroundings.

Such influences—perhaps with hints of the Alpine chalet and the verandas of Anglo-Indian houses—converged in the Bungalow, a distinctly American house popular across the country from 1900 to 1930. Despite geographical variations, this casual style maintained a broad, overhanging roof, broken with gables and

What could put a friendlier face on a street than a lineup of quaint cottages, above, complete with Carpenter Gothic details—angles and scroll-sawed trim?

dormers, that sloped down to a shady front porch framed by massive corner supports of wood or rough-hewn stone. The open-plan interior eliminated a center hall, and a boldly scaled fireplace was often used to anchor the design. Exteriors tended toward natural wood, browns, greens, creams, and russet reds.

The Bungalow was not a high-style architect's creation but, rather, a sturdy staple. From the late nineteenth century on, a builder could purchase construction-ready architectural plans for one of these basic houses for a few dollars. He

Massive, rough-finished walls in natural materials make this seaside bungalow seem one with its setting.

could even place a mail order for a whole house, complete with ready-cut lumber and siding, windows, utilities, paint, and interior trims. Between 1906 and the 1930s, Sears Roebuck, Montgomery Ward, Aladdin Home Company in Michigan, and many local firms sold thousands of basic, though ready-to-

customize, Bungalows, "Capes," and Colonials.

During the Roaring '20s and the more chastened Depression era, architects experimented with stripped-down modernism. Yet the majority of homes built at the time still hewed to traditional styles, often in sturdy and graceful renditions. After the ebulliently decorative Queen Anne houses came the simpler, more dignified Colonial Revival style, which has been a staple of American country home-building to the present day.

During the early twentieth century, the West Coast, the Southwest, and Florida rediscovered their Spanish roots with haciendas of stuccoed concrete block detailed with wrought iron and bright tilework. East Coast architects, however, waxed nostalgic for the region's Colonial clapboard farmhouses, Georgian manors, and Dutch fieldstone dwellings. An eclectic approach to architecture and design also revived country styles from other shores, such as the English half-timbered Tudor house and the French Provincial villa.

Design writers James T. Massey and Shirley Maxwell use the term "Builder Style" to designate the many houses built from 1895 to the 1930s, which defy adherence to a particular style. They note four categories:

- **Homesteads** tend to be long and narrow. The gable faces forward to hint at Greek Revival style.
- **Foursquares** are broader and more horizontal with references to the eighteenth century's Georgian forms.
- **Bungalows** share the characteristic low, overhanging, often dormered roofs and front porches, but they may borrow details from other regional styles.
- **Cottages** share the Bungalow's compactness, minus the heavy roofline. They may be enhanced with airier porches and dormers.

While builders often rendered these houses with minimal detail and an eye to economy, the authors still describe these structures as "pleasant spaces generally in pleasant neighborhoods."

Despite their traditional exteriors, early twentieth-century houses took a new direction with open floor plans that put the kitchen at the center of the household. Architects designed houses with more windows that opened more freely to natural light and exterior views.

Such openness was at the heart of another unique American house style, the Ranch, which was based loosely on a romanticized view of the Old West. Set amid

Design History at a Glance

Early American
(1640 to the early 1700s)
One-story log structures; rough timber framing; steep roofs; small casement windows; plank doors

Colonial
(early to mid 1700s)
Two or one-and-a-half stories; steep gabled roofs or sloped saltbox roofs; multipane double-hung windows; brick and clapboard siding; wrought-iron hardware

Georgian
(1740 to 1790)
Low rooflines; symmetrical facades of brick or clapboard; centered, paneled doors with pediments or porticoes; bold, neoclassical details such as heavy brackets, shutters, or arched Palladian-style windows

Federal
(1790 to 1830)
Refined neoclassical ornamentation such as delicate carving, medallions, and fanlights; tall windows; fine brickwork; rounded or oval decorative windows

Greek Revival
(1820 to 1860)
Greek temple forms such as columns and triangular pediments over door-ways; a front colonnade or porch; dentil or Greek-key carved moldings; tall windows

Gothic Revival
(1830 to 1875)
Tall, sharp-peaked rooflines; gables; turrets; windows with pointed arches; diamond-paned windows; gingerbread scrollwork trim along the eaves

Italianate Revival
(1840 to 1890)
A low-peaked or hipped roof; heavy brackets along over-hanging eaves; arched windows; porches; carved stairs

Queen Anne
(1870 to 1910)
Picturesque details; multipaned windows; mixed materials; deco-rative shingles; large porches; bays; towers; multiangled rooflines; stained glass

Colonial Revival
(1890 to present)
Restrained neoclassical orna-ment; pediments; columns; a compact, boxlike shape; pilasters; shutters; a symmetrical facade; dormers

Bungalow
(1890s to 1930s)
One or one-and-a-half stories; a low-overhanging roof; a full-width front porch; wide dormers; natural materials, such as dark-stained wood

A garden, rich with gates and arbors, is always changing, yet integral to the house's character.

the classic Cape Cods and Colonials of the post–World War II housing boom, Ranches established themselves on inexpensive land beyond the city limits. Single-story, flat-roofed, wide-windowed, and open throughout, these homes seemed the last word in modernity. Yet today the Ranch has retreated far enough in our design history to warrant nostalgia among baby boomers. The sunlit, streamlined interiors of these houses can provide an unobtrusive background to an easy, eclectic country decor.

DECORATIVE INFLUENCES

The architecture of a house is often the jumping-off point for its interior decoration. In a Craftsman Bungalow with a river-rock facade, wallpaper with a little sprigged print may be fussy and off-key, while a darker, bold floral—though not strictly of the period—may appear perfectly in tune. In the same way, "homespun" will be too rustic for a classic Federal manor, yet a rich wood will look appropriate while retaining an country appeal. Similarly, a sleek ranch house lends itself to retro-cottage freshness more than a Craftsman aura. These architectural cues, taken as suggestions, can be a fertile source of country decorating inspiration. ✍

4

COUNTRY BACKDROPS
Walls and Windows

odern design broke with long-standing tradition when it presented a room as a clean-lined white box. Prior to the mid-twentieth century, texture and dimension brought richness to walls and floors. Some of this character was inherent in the timeless materials and building methods: even the simplest workingman's cabin or frontier farmhouse owed its warmth to timber framework, wide-plank floors, and rough whitewash over hand-troweled plaster. But people are rarely content with simplicity, and our ancestors enthusiastically paneled, painted, papered, and carpeted their rooms with color and pattern.

WALL FINISHES

Colonists brought with them Europe's ancient *wattle and daub* construction, with walls made of interwoven branches and straw covered in clay and whitewashed inside. This gave way to wooden lath coated with multiple layers of plaster, which remained the standard interior wall until World War II. In the postwar building boom, the faster, cheaper application of gypsum drywall with taped-and-sanded joints became the standard smooth background.

Specialized craftspeople can still build genuine plaster walls. However, one popular method to achieve this look is by veneer plastering: applying a cover coat of plaster to specialized drywall to give it a solid, monolithic appearance without a hint of seams or "nail pops." Though more expensive and time-consuming than installing and finishing standard drywall, veneer plastering produces a sturdier surface and eliminates the dust generated by sanding.

Another way to simulate the look of old plaster walls is with tinted joint compound. Skim-coat the entire surface of the drywall, and create a textured effect by using a brush or trowel. Special paint can also make a badly taped or slightly battered surface look artistically textural.

WALLPAPER

One popular option has always been wallpaper, then as now. In the late eighteenth century, well-to-do American colonists prized imported wallpapers with bold designs, especially hand-painted mural papers from China. During the nineteenth century, machine-printing on continuous rolls made wallpaper affordable for more people. Patterns tended to be realistic, brightly colored, and scaled small

A documentary wallpaper of exotic birds and flowers, opposite, brings a lively period flavor to a formal Colonial dining room.

With wide-plank floors, plaster walls, and heavy woodwork painted in a deep, somber tone, an entry, below, in a center-hall Colonial offers a dignified welcome.

Walls, above, covered in crisp stripes of cool blue and white exude a sweet simplicity.

Whitewashed walls and woodwork, opposite, covered in durable, richly hued paint present a practical and time-honored finish.

enough for printing using a copper roller. Manufacturers made flocked designs by applying shredded velvet to adhesive-coated paper. In reaction to this flood of machine-made wallpaper, "art" manufacturers and designers, such as England's William Morris, focused on flat, bold, stylized motifs or Japanese inspirations produced, once again, with time-consuming block-printing.

In today's wallpaper market, you can have it all—florals in bold bouquets or tiny sprigs, dramatic or low-key geometric patterns, or easy-to-coordinate stripes and checks. Some wallpapers successfully emulate the texture of fabric or painted faux finishes. Heavily embossed patterns, usually designed for painting, look nostalgic and can conceal less-than-perfect walls. Many wallpapers coordinate with a line of paint, borders, and fabrics.

Several major manufacturers produce motifs that derive from antique examples, often under a licensing agreement with a historical society or museum. For versatility, the design may be spun into a range of colorations along with the original "documentary" colors. A few specialty companies make a limited number of hand-screened or hand-blocked papers in exact reproductions of historic ones. While these wallpapers can be striking in their authenticity, they usually require professional installation and special paste.

When selecting a wallpaper pattern, be sure that it is in proportion to the size of the room. However, a bold design can add a sense of drama to a small room, while a subtle motif can be exactly what's needed to visually scale down space that is too grand to be cozy. Try out a pattern before making an expensive investment in wallpaper. Bring home a good-size sample, or buy one roll. Tape it onto a wall, and view it in the room's natural and artificial light. Keep the sample in place for a few days to see how the pattern wears on you and whether it gets along with other elements in the room.

PAINTED HISTORY

For centuries, people whitewashed the interiors of humble houses as well as the utility areas of grand homes with lime. When walls became dirty and smudged with soot from smoke and lamp oil, they were simply recoated. Sometimes people added tint to the whitewash using earth pigments, such as red or yellow ocher clays, for a hint of color.

Because the whitewash would flake or rub off, people preferred paint, a more durable coating for paneling, trim, and furniture. Prior to the nineteenth century, people made their own paint or obtained it from itinerants who carried powdered pigments with them from place to place. These pigments included expensive imported Prussian blue or bright verdigris green (the result of oxidized copper), as well as cheaper domestic earth pigments, ready to mix with a locally available liquid binder. For wealthy clients, painters mixed the pigments with an emulsion of linseed oil and egg yolk to make a durable, slightly glossy finish. In rural, less prosperous regions, they mixed pigments with lime and readily available skim milk or buttermilk. The resulting milk paint dried to a smooth, rich-tinted matte finish. The caustic lime breaks down proteins in milk, re-forming them into a tough bonded coating, which still survives on antique pieces today. Such homemade paints persisted in rural locations long after premixed products became available in the late nineteenth century.

If you crave authenticity in your country settings, you can purchase whitewash or milk paint from a few specialty manufacturers. But the majority of today's interior paints are either alkyd or latex products. Alkyd paints are lustrous and hard-wearing but toxic and combustible. They require good ventilation when drying, special disposal, and a solvent for cleanup. Latex paints, which now rival alkyds' durability and textural range, dry quickly and clean up easily with soap and water. Most people find latex paints easier to use.

Color Selection. Color tends to amplify when you use it in quantity, and it's hard to imagine an entire finished room from a tiny paint chip. If you're planning a bold color choice, buy a small quantity of paint and cover a large section of primed drywall. View it by natural and artificial light, especially during the hours when you typically use the room. Try to examine it against a neutral background, because a white contrast may make the color appear unrealistically bright.

Rugged timber beams, above, and bright white moldings interplay with the rich blue walls that flow from room to room.

Walls subtly patterned in a patchwork of creamy tones, opposite, enhance the striking geometry of a lofty, rustic space. Painted chairs enliven it with color.

PAINTED EFFECTS

The traveling housepainters of earlier centuries, often trained in English, Scandinavian, or German decorative traditions, routinely produced faux finishes such as graining or marbling or patterns inspired by nature—fruit, flowers, animals, and birds. If asked, they'd also turn a hand to painting a portrait, producing many charming early American examples. Special painted finishes, a staple in early American houses, persisted into the late nineteenth century on the frontier, where wallpaper and other decorative devices were hard to come by.

Painted effects bring that sense of history with them into today's country rooms. Such visually rich treatments are generally used sparingly to avoid competing with each other.

Decorative painting can be loosely divided into three categories:

- **Pictorial effects** that add recognizable motifs with stencils or freehand painting
- **Faux finishes** that emulate natural materials, such as wood grain or stone speckling
- **Broken-color, or antiquing, finishes** that suggest the character-enhancing streaking and mottling reminiscent of vintage painted or whitewashed walls or furniture

While certain painted finishes demand considerable artistic skill, many are within reach of the careful amateur guided by detailed directions that are available from specialized books, paint manufacturers' Web sites, and in-store literature. Preformulated glazes are available for specific effects, although many painters make their own glazes by judiciously thinning and tinting standard paints. Even professionals practice a new technique and try out color combinations first on a primed piece of hardboard. If a large blank wall is intimidating, an inexpensive furniture piece or a craft object may be the best place to hone a new painting skill.

PICTURE-PRETTY TECHNIQUES

Numerous painting techniques don't require a lot of skill, just a little practice. Following are brief descriptions of some the most popular painted decorative finishes that are enjoying a renaissance today.

Stenciling. This technique achieves a repeated design by applying paint through the cutout sections of a template. It is an ancient craft applied to walls and furni-

A hazy, broken-color painted finish, above, lends a library a sense of contemplative antiquity.

Painted elements are often effective in small doses, such as this stair-well's scattering of stenciled leaves, opposite top, or a border on a floor, opposite bottom.

ACCENT PIECES

Don't forget the details.
Decorative painting can extend to
lamps and lamp shades, roller shades, hatboxes,
wastebaskets, storage tins,
or shelves.

ture that flourished again as a folk art in eighteenth- and nineteenth-century American houses.

Today you have a head start because precut stencils are readily available. They range from the simplest tulip to ornate, multicolor motifs harking back to the turn-of-the-twentieth-century Arts and Crafts era, when stenciling had a revival for its idiosyncratic, handmade appeal. But if that isn't enough, you can cut your own stencils on acetate or a stencil-card with a motif from your imagination or borrowed from wallpaper or fabric.

Stenciling paint is thick. Apply it with light, pouncing dabs using an almost dry brush or small sponge. The finished effect can be naive and flat, delicately shaded, or enhanced with hand-painted details.

Stamping or Block Printing. This craft also achieves simple, graphic pictures using a rubber or wooden stamp. You can purchase a stamp with a ready-made raised motif, or you can carve your own design into a prepared block, a firm sponge, or even a potato. While certain irregularity is desirable, you can touch up any sloppy edges with a brush. Block prints best suit a small, flat surface, such as a window frame or a furniture piece.

Trompe L'Oeil. This technique is a visual trick consisting of skillfully painted three-dimensional illusions. It demands artistic ability to realistically evoke a window vista or a tabletop scattered with objects. Lacking that, you may enjoy planning a simple, flat mural or copying a picture. To transfer an image to the wall, enlarge the picture on a photocopier, and then draw a grid over it. Lightly sketch a scaled-up version of the grid on the wall, and then copy the picture in increments.

Trompe l'oeil artistry, above, creates the illusion of a pastoral view, framed in rough stone walls.

FAUX FINISHES

To create a faux finish, an artist uses paint to emulate the look of a natural material such as a particular wood or stone, with its many variations.

Marbling. Fine marbling entails a number of decorative painting techniques, with darker and lighter color-washed streaks of glaze topped with delicate veining applied with feathers and special brushes. Skilled painters may also mimic the look of other stones, such as speckled granite or malachite. Faux-stone techniques are usually reserved for small decorative touches on a mantel, trimwork, or tabletop.

Graining. Another faux finish, graining dresses up inexpensive softwoods by mimicking the strong decorative grain patterns of fine mahogany, oak, or burled walnut. To achieve the effect, first apply a tinted base coat, and then follow up with a glaze. With special combs and short-bristled brushes, drag through the still-wet glaze to lay in the grain and the requisite swirls and whorls. In *vinegar graining,* touches of vinegar pool up the glaze to create the "bird's eye" of decorative maple veneer.

Some graining is realistic, but many country pieces are "fantasy grained" in livelier colors and broader strokes for a lighthearted effect. Such graining borders on an abstract *broken-color finish.*

BROKEN-COLOR EFFECTS

Broken-color finishes add depth and variety to flat color across the expanse of a wall. Begin with a fully dried base coat, and apply over this a thinned, translucent glaze, which can be manipulated. Such effects can be a creative cure for a paint job that didn't turn out as planned. A closely related base color and glaze, such as

Hand-painted fruit-laden branches, above, layer another pattern above a display of ceramics.

a light and slightly deeper tone of the same color, add up to a subtle effect, generally easier for a novice to control. Using two contrasting colors emboldens the pattern and requires greater precision in the application.

Combing. A playful, bold, and less formal version of graining, combing is a perfect country finish. Using wide-toothed steel, rubber, or metal combs, or homemade grainers made with notched cardboard or a notched squeegee, you can manipulate the wet, thick glaze and comb it into waves, zigzags, overlapped semicircles, checkerboards, or plaids.

Sponging. To use this technique, layer on glaze or paint (or pull off the medium while it is still wet) with a dampened natural sponge for an effect that can be crisply patterned or soft and muted. Beginners often favor this fairly quick and easy effect. The important thing to remember is to keep the sponge damp—not wet—and to replace a sponge that has become saturated with paint. You can layer several colors, although the cumulative effect should be kept soft and cloudlike.

Ragging. This craft is similar to sponging, but it involves handling the paint or glaze with crumpled lint-free rags or cheesecloth for a bold pattern. You can use the technique to apply or remove the color. A variation on the process is rag-rolling, which involves manipulating the medium with a rolled up, sausage-shaped rag.

Stippling. To stipple a surface, you'll need a stiff brush either to apply glaze to the dry undercoat in a pouncing motion or to jab a wet glaze layer for a speckled finish. You can use any stiff-bristled brush or a stippling brush designed specifically for this

Hazy golden walls of broken-color painting, opposite, fashion a low-key background, ready to go with a variety of bright table settings.

For a bedroom, below, the painted effects are kept restful and simple and in soft tints of the owner's favorite colors.

purpose. Different brushes create hazy or crisp patterns; either one takes a sure, practiced hand to keep a consistent look over a large area.

Color-washing. Giving a subtle dappled finish, color-washing offers an excellent camouflage for slightly uneven walls. Apply a thin, filmy glaze lightly and randomly over the walls in overlapping strokes. Or use a roller to coat the wall, and then work the glaze with a damp sponge or a soft, dry brush. It takes several coats to achieve the proper coverage. With warm, closely related tones such as gold over dark yellow or two tints of terra-cotta, color-washing creates an antique, rustic, uneven stone effect that's ideal for Old World–inspired country settings.

Dragging. Pulling a long-haired brush through a wet glaze in long, smooth strokes is key to this technique, which is also called *strié*. The finished look is elegant and silken, but it takes a skilled hand.

Spattering. A spattered finish coats a surface with random sprays or dots of paint flicked from a brush or a bundle of fine twigs. It's easier to apply to horizontal surfaces and may take some practice to achieve a reasonably even coating.

A FEW MORE ILLUSIONS

Distressing is another way to give a painted finish the look of age and wear. On a furniture piece, you can easily create the appearance of years of use. Apply two heavy coats of paint in contrasting colors. After the paint dries, rub it with coarse steel wool to reveal the color of the first coat and even some of the natural hue of the wood. Make natural-looking wear patterns with the steel wool at corners and edges and around the handles. You can "dirty" the effect with dark wax. Most paint and craft stores and home centers offer a variety of products for theatrical aging, such as antiqued or crackled finishes that can integrate a brash new piece into a mellow, slightly worn setting.

Pickling, or *liming,* involves rubbing white pigment into the grain of oak or pine for a subtle lightening effect that allows some of the wood grain to show through. The technique originated in the sixteenth century with caustic lime finishes

that were used to protect wood from insects. By the eighteenth century, it was a favorite decorative finish. You can buy special pickling pastes or produce a similar effect by rubbing thinned white latex paint into the grain of the wood, working over a small area at a time before the paint dries.

DRESSING THE COUNTRY WINDOW

In the room's background, the window is always one standout feature. Some period windows, such as the oval *cameo,* round *bull's-eye,* or arched *eyebrow,* are small and strictly decorative. Let them remain unadorned. Unless privacy is an issue, a large, magnificent window may look its best unadorned as well. Remember, however, that a big sunny window can look like a cold, dark void come nighttime. If you use the room in the evening, you might have a reason for

With modern paints, you can pickle wood surfaces, such as these shutters, above, to bring a classic vintage look to a room.

With mottled, artistically "distressed" walls, opposite, a stairwell takes on the charm of an Old World villa.

Challenging Windows

few houses have the "perfect" window that fits exactly into everyone's decorating plans. But the right dressing can help reproportion a window that's an awkward size or shape. Here are a few examples.

- Resize an overlarge picture window, often a later addition to an older home, and make it look in better proportion to a cozy room with a streamlined, sill-length curtain. A contrasting valance will help visually break up the height.
- Visually lengthen short, choppy windows by installing the rod above the window trim and hiding the gap with a long valance. Match the topping to the curtains to create a long, smooth flow to the floor.
- Unify dissimilar windows with similar window treatments that share the same top and bottom lines.
- Widen a narrow window by extending the rod past the sides, and use opaque rather than sheer curtains to hide the opening's exact edges.

Don't forget that a window treatment can play an important role in the décor of a room. A romantic bedroom calls out for lush chintz and a dignified parlor for broadcloth drapes with a shaped cornice. In general, the style or type of window treatment typically coordinates with the room's character. Yet this rule can be tweaked to suit your decorating needs. For example, if a rustic room feels heavy and dark, maybe it needs an airy bit of lace at the window. When a room of Victorian velvet upholstery appears too formal or stuffy, try a sprigged muslin curtain to easily transform the space with a cottage-fresh and casual ambiance.

A lightweight makeshift swag, right, romances a rustic room.

A single window, opposite, gains importance when the curtain rod is extended across the wall.

installing a suitable window treatment. But a better reason is that fabrics soften the hard-edged opening with color and pattern that may even take the spotlight in the room's design.

Whether you choose custom or ready-made window dressings, here are a few steps toward zeroing in on a suitable choice.

smart steps

one **Consider the practicalities.** Perhaps you're looking for a window treatment to create privacy, control glare, or add insulation. Do you seek to frame the view or to obscure it? Will you need to open and close the window (and covering) frequently? Consider also how your choice of treatment will fit the daily scene. In a busy passageway, puddled full-length curtains are impractical. In a room open to a busy street, delicate dry-clean-only sheers are bound to get grimy. And in a kitchen, anything you can't wash is out of the question.

two **Don't discount the decorative possibilities of hard treatments.** Hard treatments—shades, blinds, or shutters—can be easily adjusted to control light and privacy. Plus, they have a long history in everyday rooms, especially prior to the greater availability of fabrics from the middle of the nineteenth century onward. Wood is the most sympathetic material for a country window, although dark-wood shutters and blinds significantly reduce

Mix or match? A bamboo shade, left, on one window and a curtain on another enliven this cozy reading corner.

A handsome window, opposite, can remain uncovered to show off its architectural character.

Sheer panels, right, neutral and light-filtering, *adapt to many country settings, casual or formal. Tie tabs add charming detail. The slight puddling of the fabric onto the floor lends a grace note to the overall effect.*

the amount of intrusive sunlight. Interior shutters become part of the architecture, much in the manner of moldings.

Miniblinds and newer varieties of pleated and cellular shades lean toward a modern look, but in a neutral hue they easily blend into the wall color or the topping fabric. So you don't have to rule them out of your country scheme.

three **Decide how structured you want the window treatment to look.** Although some design purists insist that the only correct term is "curtain," most people use the word drapery when referring to floor-length, pleated lined panels mounted with hooks on a traverse rod. Heading styles may include simple pinch pleats or shapely goblet, boxed, or smocked pleats. For the dressiest look, layer draperies over sheers, and top the treatment with an overlaying shaped cornice or a valance. But remember, draperies are formal, grand, and often of a period.

In the same spirit, curtains typically refer to loosely structured, light, unlined or lightly lined fabrics or sheer lace panels that hang from a fixed rod with tabs, ties, or rings. These styles are more at home in casual country rooms.

Between hard and soft window treatments is an appealing middle ground with decorative forms of shades, such as flouncy Austrian or balloon versions and more tailored flat-panel Roman shades. Today, with a kit, you can easily fuse your favorite fabric onto simple roller blinds, too.

Another lively component to consider is the range of valances, cornices, and swags to top a window. These may conceal the hardware of structured draperies or soften the straight lines of simple shades and blinds. Or they can be used alone to add a dash of curve and color without obscuring the light or the breeze. 🕸

Spurs attached to leather straps hang from a wooden pole, above, and are decoration enough to emphasize this tiny window.

5

INTERIOR FEATURES
With Country Character

Perhaps for the sheer pleasure of it, or maybe instinctively, people have always decorated. Our eighteenth- and nineteenth-century ancestors took particular pride in the elements that brought beauty and character into their homes: finely joined paneling, turned trim and carved moldings, and ornate brickwork. If your house has such inherent memorable features, your decorating decisions can celebrate them. But if it lacks architectural character, there are things you can do to add it. In this chapter, you'll find ideas for windows, floors, stairs, fireplaces, and detailed trimwork.

ALL THE TRIMMINGS

In addition to decoration, architectural moldings serve practical ends—covering gaps and settling where walls meet floors, ceilings, and openings, and protecting doorways and walls from careless knocks. Such utilitarian aims, which you can easily achieve with a plain strip of wood, don't account for history's astonishing variety of distinctive architectural trimmings.

In vintage Colonial farmhouses, you can see the ceiling beams' strong horizontal lines repeated in a simple chair-rail molding intended to protect the plaster. In elegant country homes, where heavy crown moldings implied status, finely paneled wainscoting sometimes extended into a full wall of woodwork around the fireplace.

Early in the nineteenth century, Neoclassical influences made trimmings light and "Grecian," with intricately detailed friezes, ceiling medallions, and scalloped niches. Outside of the centers of fashion, simpler details still reigned—in the farmhouse with its open beams, sturdy tongue-and-groove wainscoting, and peg rails for handy storage. Built-in corner cabinets offered both storage and display space for items such as fine china.

As the nineteenth century progressed, architectural ornament proliferated, even in fairly modest houses. Immigrant woodworkers from Europe competed with the rise of machine-cut "gingerbread" or factory-molded trims of composite materials. The era's fashionably tall ceilings didn't seem towering when they divided, as fashion dictated, into at least three levels.

- An upper frieze of molded plaster or a wallpaper border installed below a heavy crown molding
- The lower wall, or dado, which was paneled, papered, or covered in heavily embossed synthetic material, known, then and now, by such names as "Anaglypta" or "Lincrusta"
- The wall in between, which was painted or treated with wallpaper and further sectioned off with picture molding

By the turn of the twentieth century, in the Arts and Crafts manner, moldings became bolder and simpler, wearing natural finishes to play up the wood grain. Builders framed doorways and windows with plain

Strong and simple, the wide-plank floors and the plain moldings exemplify this house's Colonial heritage. A double-wide door frames the view of neatly composed rooms accented in red and blue.

lengths of wood, adding corner plinth blocks sometimes carved with stylized rosettes. But by the end of World War II, with the proliferation of tract houses, almost all architectural detail became passé.

If your country house lacks architectural interest, and you are looking for ways to add it, follow these steps.

smart steps

one **Look to the existing house for both inspiration and limits.** While classic architectural features decorate the facades of many new houses today,

White paneling extending to the lofty ceiling and light-filled doors and windows fashion a clean, airy country background.

they are typically nonexistent once you get past the front door. In other instances, former renovations have stripped the interiors of some older homes of their original interesting decorative features. In these cases, you can refer to exterior details for style inspiration and guidance. Boldly scaled crown moldings are compatible with a center-hall Colonial, and a river-rock fireplace is perfect for a Craftsman bungalow, for example.

There may be instances when you need to compromise with the existing design of a house. Colonial moldings will not make a house with vaulted ceilings and lots

Architectural features also meet practical needs. A Shaker-simple pegged shelf, bottom, displays vintage clothing but could also serve for basic storage.

PLASTIC MOLDINGS AND TRIM

Architectural trims molded in modern polymers are reasonably priced, lightweight, easy to cut and install, and ready to paint or faux-grain. They offer remarkable detail in historically accurate reproductions and can achieve an elaborate profile in one easy piece.

A few innovative ideas:

Shallow recessed domes that you can install in a standard-height ceiling, leaving the dome rim to cover the rough opening

Columns cast in fiberglass/resin composites, with stone dust in the mix for a natural look. These hollow columns can conceal ductwork, wiring, and load-bearing supports

Niches that add instant display space

Plastic's drawbacks? It's less durable and might not serve as well as wood. Its rigidity makes it prone to gaps if the building settles over time.

of glass appear charming or old-fashioned—they'll merely look odd. In this case, keeping the background plain and unobtrusive and concentrating on furnishings with a clean-line country flavor can create an appealing modern adaptation of country style.

two **Research historical styles.** If you live in an older home, or wish to re-create a period atmosphere, you may enjoy learning about an era's typical colors, patterns, and building practices. Take advantage of the library, museums, and local historical societies. If you live amid houses of similar vintage, your neighbors may be willing to talk about their decorating efforts. (Getting them to stop might be another matter.)

three **Scope out current resources for vintage flavor.** Many building-product, furniture, and paint companies reproduce period details or loose interpretations. Explore how modern materials can make it easy to achieve certain antique looks. Research Web sites, which sometimes attract visitors with fascinating historical background.

four **Establish priorities to fit your budget.** Changing the windows or laying a new floor can transform a room. But will such big-budget items leave enough money for the other things you're planning? If you relocate later, you might be less interested in making structural changes than in acquiring furnishings that can move with you.

Particularly in a genuinely old house (as opposed to one that just looks old), unglamorous work on the mechanical and structural systems must come first. Nothing is less fun than backtracking in your decorating efforts—for example, tearing through the expensive hand-blocked wallpaper to replace the plumbing.

Installing moldings and trim has become a fairly straightforward project, given the array of products available from home centers, hardware stores, architectural salvage shops, specialized millwork shops, and woodworkers who specialize in custom work. Wood is the traditional option. Pressed-wood moldings are inexpensive but dense, heavy, and fragile.

As for solid-wood moldings, hardwoods such as oak and cherry are treasured for their fine grain when stained and varnished. Less expensive woods, such as pine and birch, are at their best wearing a painted finish—a look that is more authentic to humbler rooms. For an elaborate built-up treatment, combine several styles.

For a classic look, install wainscoting. You can do this with a kit of precut planks or more easily with scored 32- to 36-inch-tall panels. The panels are finished with simulated wood grain or with genuine wood veneers.

Moldings and purchased millwork can do more than cover the room's seams. Consider their potential to transform an interior.

Manufacturers offer literature with ideas and instructions on measuring and installation. Plaster is architecturally correct for Neoclassical styles. You can buy today's "plasterwork" by the running foot and in precast niches and medallions.

A WORLD OF WINDOWS

Windows determine a room's outlook, both in the real and metaphorical sense. A cottage's small casements exude coziness, while the glass expanses of a modern timber-framed residence play up its openness.

Glass is an ancient material, but flat panes are a relatively late innovation. To make window glass, early glassblowers would slice the clear, molten bubble off the blowpipe and spin it until the opened bubble flapped out flat. Antique glass still shows the concentric "bulls-eye" rings that result from this method.

In the past, greased paper or cloth covered the openings in many rough

A simple twelve-over-twelve muntined window in natural wood, above, presents a history-rich feature, harking back to an era when glass was costly, even in small panes.

An exquisite decorative window, opposite, brightens this stairway.

dwellings because glass was expensive, even in small pieces. Side-opening casements, often with small diamond-shaped panes, were the first operational windows. Double-hung windows, introduced in the 1700s, eclipsed them with nine or twelve panes per sash, divided by wide muntins. Later Neoclassical styles encouraged thinner muntins and fewer, larger panes, as well as distinctive arched-top Palladian-inspired windows. Decorative windows in ovals, circles, and half-circles offered other graceful touches.

Picturesque Victorian country styles depended on lively windows, including a return to Colonial multipane sashes, quaint "eyebrow" windows, "lancet" windows with sharp-pointed arches, and a proliferation of stained glass. The era's bay windows are an enchanting addition, bringing in lots of light and sometimes extra floor space.

Historic wooden windows stand forward as strong, hand-crafted elements that invigorate a country home's surroundings, above.

ASSESSING EXISTING WINDOWS

Because windows open to the elements, they're prone to deterioration. If your windows are old, your first impulse, encouraged by the current marketplace and rightly placed concerns about energy-efficiency, may be toward replacement. Yet repair may be more cost-effective. This is true if the windows are distinctive, because custom-made historically accurate ones may be prohibitively pricey.

Reclaiming a decrepit wooden window may involve a simple sash-replacement kit or more laborious patching of decayed wood with a fungicide and epoxy compound. If an older window is still reasonably sound, you can fit it with weatherstripping and unobtrusive storm units to make it almost as energy-efficient as some modern versions.

If you want to change the window, you'll have to sort through many products in vinyl, aluminum, and wood, the traditional choice. Specifications by the National Fenestration Rating Council (NFRC) provide a yardstick to compare performance among brands. Get estimates from various suppliers, with a clear understanding of the warranties, the materials, and the cost of labor.

HOME AND HEARTH

With or without a fire, a fireplace always seems to be the natural center of a room. Perhaps it touches upon a deep-seated feeling about fire's importance in our history. Or maybe the glow, the aroma, and the crackle of flames simply appeal to our senses. Our ancestors had to cope with dangerous fireplaces. Early on in the American colonies, ordinances mandated brick fireboxes. Fire wardens checked new buildings for such safety measures and tolled bells for "curfew," meaning "cover fire," the last step in safely settling the household down for the night.

A fireplace is a natural focal point, so the owners of this one, below, made it a display area for a collection of antique kitchenwares and vintage advertising paraphernalia.

Drafts and heat loss posed other concerns. The Rumford fireplace first appeared in 1796. It soon became state of the art. Tall and shallow, it features a streamlined throat at the chimney base that draws smoke more efficiently and deflects more radiant heat from the masonry firebox into the room. Writer Henry David Thoreau named the Rumford fireplace, plaster walls, and venetian blinds as comforts that his contemporaries took for granted. Fireplace designers today are still exploring and applying Rumford's original designs (misapplied by many early interpreters) to make a more efficiently burning fireplace. The style's tall, elegant line looks particularly fine in a room with high ceilings.

Conventional wood-burning masonry fireplaces are an extravagance in modern times, however, and local building departments may even prohibit them in some cases. If your house has an old fireplace or you want to add a new one, it's worth investigating the technology of today's energy-smart prefabricated fireplaces, some of which burn alternative types of fuel. Gas-fueled models called direct-vent fireplaces don't even require a chimney, because they are vented directly to the outdoors through the wall or ceiling. Simulated logs eliminate the labor of carrying and replenishing firewood, building fires, and cleaning up, but they lack the variety, crackle, and aroma of wood.

A rugged brick fireplace, above, is suitably framed by painted woodwork and a classic portrait.

Heat-resistant blue-and-white ceramic tile, opposite, adds a distinctive finishing detail to this fireplace surround.

STOVES

When cast-iron heating stoves debuted in the late 1700s, people embraced them as more-effective heaters, if a bit less romantic than an open hearth. Today, the Environmental Protection Agency strictly regulates woodstoves. Modern woodstoves minimize emissions with catalytic converters or newer noncatalytic systems that recirculate the smoke and burn it before it exits. Most stoves still have homey cast-iron or potbellied styling; many have large viewing windows as well. You can also enclose a stove within a surround of brick, tile, or stone to give it the look of a fireplace, especially if you add a mantel.

ACCOMPANIMENTS TO THE FIRE

Naturally, the fireplace should epitomize the room's style. A beam of aged wood and a brick or river-rock facing might suit a rustic room, while a carved wooden mantel and surround might be the centerpiece of a prosperous farmhouse. Heatproof ceramic tile has long served as fireplace cladding in evocative patterns from rough terra-cotta to dainty blue-and-white delftware or hand-molded Craftsman tiles in rich iridescent glazes. During the Victorian era, thematic "hearth sets" of printed tiles displayed the passing seasons or scenes from Shakespeare.

Beyond the mantel as a display area, don't overlook the decorative power of fireplace or stove-side accessories. They might include

- Log carriers and racks
- Painted or wrought-iron fireplace screens
- Brass fenders
- Painted matchboxes
- Brass fireplace tools for a more formal look or wrought-iron pieces for a rustic effect

This seldom-used fireplace, above, is dressed for show with a draftblocking hand-painted fire board.

Dominating the interior of a soaring post-andbeam cabin, opposite, an unusual rustic stairway combines blunt squarejointed outlines with balusters of twining branches.

A firebox minus the fire can look like a cold, dark hole. That's hardly an appealing sight in an otherwise cozy country room. Aside from keeping a fire lit all year long, there are things you can do to make it an attention-grabbing frame for a number of decorative items. Try adding

- A cast-iron fireback
- A dried floral arrangement
- A hand-painted or embroidered fire board
- A painted firewood box
- A grouping of candles

STAIRWAYS

In space-tight colonial-American houses, stairs tended to be narrow, steep, and sharply turned. As houses became grander, so did the stairways. In the classic center-hall farmhouse, stairs are often the first thing a visitor sees straight upon entering the front door; in antebellum plantation houses, stairs may wind into a graceful curve within the front hall.

Though typically an afterthought, stairways can generously reward decorating efforts. Often prominent in the house's public areas, their dynamic diagonal lines draw the eye upward. This is a short-stay area where a bold finish won't grow tiresome, yet it's small enough to keep subtle effects from becoming lost. The stairs' risers make a particularly prominent display. You can tile them or dress them with a decorative paint finish or a stenciled design to present either a repeated motif or rows of related images.

Wide stairways can be prime showcases for artwork, perhaps with a diagonal run of pictures on the wall or small collectibles grouped along the stairs' edge outside the railing. A generous landing might hold shelves or a small handcrafted chair. Also think about other decorative notions.

- Brass stair rods locking down a low-pile runner at the bottom of each riser can be an appealing embellishment. Thrifty Victorian housewives shifted the carpeting up or down periodically to even out the wear.
- Molding or a carved medallion applied to the outside of the stringer adds an elegant ornamental touch.
- Big, attractive baskets near the top and bottom of the stairs can handily gather stuff to take up or down on the next trip.

SMART TIP

STAIRS

Stairs can be dangerous, so stick to nonslip surfaces, keep handrails secure and preferably mounted on both sides, tack down loose runners, and never leave items, collectibles or otherwise, in the path of traffic.

FLOORS

While facing a tougher physical challenge than any other surface, a floor also carries a lot of the room's sense of style. And for a country room, flooring should be fashioned from natural materials, or at least a convincing imitation. Ceramic tile, made of elemental clays, can fill that role. In fact, ceramic floors can appear throughout the house. (See the discussion on tile in Chapter 9, "In the Country Kitchen," page 146.)

WOOD UNDERFOOT

Probably the most popular country flooring material is wood, whether in standard narrow strips, wide planks, or intricate parquet patterns that set a formal tone. Softwood pine and fir are less expensive, but they're also less durable than a hardwood such as oak, which is by far the most popular choice. Other less common and more expensive hardwoods offer their own distinct characteristics, such as the smooth, uniform look of maple. Wood is graded by appearance according to color, grain, and imperfections. All grades are durable, and a lower grade might provide a desirably rustic look at lower cost.

The traditional stain-and-wax finish still has its fans, willing to maintain it with periodic re-waxing and buffing. More often, today's wood floors receive a tough urethane coating (usually in a matte finish for a mellow country appearance). Urethane finishes are maintained with light damp-mopping and manufacturer-recommended cleaners. They will require refinishing every five to ten years, depending on the usage.

Increasingly, wood flooring is factory-finished for an easier installation over a greater variety of substrates; installation may even be a do-it-yourself undertaking with a prefabricated wood-floor kit. Some "engineered" wood products are thick enough to withstand sanding and recoating when the time comes. Others, including laminated products with a simulated wood-look layer, are extremely hard-wearing, but you can't refinish them later. Once one of these floors becomes worn, after about 15 years, you'll have to replace it.

DECORATING WITH WOOD

Wood is generally an easy-to-coordinate material, but you might ask some questions about how it fits into your scheme.

For example, you might wonder, "Is a wood floor a neutral background or a strong pattern in its own right?" Strongly grained narrow-strip oak is busier than wide planking with a subdued grain; intricate parquet squares are stronger still. Country rooms often mix patterns freely, but make sure the overall effect is lively rather than overpowering.

Another thing to consider is the color of the wood or the stain. Does it fit in with

To dress up a knotty wide-plank floor, above, a stencil was overlaid around the perimeter.

Translucent stains and contrasting accents give this fine-grained wood floor, opposite, the look of elegant marquetry.

the color or decorating scheme of the room? Generally, lighter wood tones seem less formal and more space-enhancing, and darker stains more elegant. Particularly fine furniture that's predominantly light or dark in color can stand out against a contrasting floor.

In earlier times, wood floors were less often seen in their natural hues. English cottage floors were sometimes rubbed with lime to repel wood-boring insects, and the light pickled look has remained popular for centuries. Or floors were painted, partly to protect but more to brighten the surroundings with stenciling and freehand motifs. Such artistry underfoot, either in opaque paints or semitransparent stains, is still a striking option for today's country settings.

But remember, in a small space a painted border may be hidden by furniture or rugs, so your efforts may not be on display. Small floors, such as in a hallway, can be captivating in an overall pattern that might grow tiresome in a big expanse.

CARPETING

Carpeting generally refers to a broadloom product that's installed wall to wall, perhaps over a rough substrate, while the term rug denotes a smaller, soft floor covering laid over a finished floor. Carpeting offers a unified visual sweep, toe-pleasing comfort, and lower noise levels.

Large, room-size rugs appeared as a fairly late development in the Western world. By the early eighteenth century, England had begun factory production of carpets at the cities of Kidderminster, Wilton, and Axminster, which lent their names to various types of utility carpeting, woven in narrow strips and sewn together to cover larger areas. In 1791, America's first carpet factory opened in Philadelphia; by the mid-1800s, such factories tripled their production with steam-driven looms while branching into more vividly patterned products. Large

A "patchwork" look and elements of Native American design give this rug, above, a unique country personality.

Texture can be found in many forms. Weathered barn siding, opposite, reclaimed from a demolition, conveys an immediate aura of age.

carpets had to be conscientiously swept (perhaps after being scattered with damp tea leaves to keep down dust) and hauled outside for beating.

Durable wool is a natural choice, but carpeting is also made of easy-care synthetic fibers in an even wider range of styles. Because wall-to-wall carpeting doesn't have strong country credentials, it's most effective when kept simple and neutral. A corded surface in a hazy sage green or a low-looped flecked tan Berber can complement any number of furnishings, while natural-fiber carpeting, such as sisal, coir, or jute, lends a summer-house informality to a room. ✺

SMART TIP

ANTIQUE WOOD

Some Country devotees crave the patina of antique, distressed lumber salvaged from a number of sources—old barns or the beams from old East Coast factories now being torn down. No grading system exists for these goods, so be sure to do business with an established supplier. Such wood is known for its distinctive characteristics, and a supplier may be able to give you a good idea of the rustic results.

6

FURNISHING YOUR HOUSE

In the Country Style

Once you've dispatched the big expanses of walls and floors, the fun of country decorating begins with dressing the space in personality-rich furniture and fabrics. Textures, patterns, and shapes bring a room to life as you compose both the overall impression of an interior and the fine details and personal touches. When you're considering what to buy and what type of furniture to use, remember that country rooms often bypass the matched suite in favor of individually chosen unmatched pieces. In fact, you may already own items that would be suitable with a bit of rethinking and minor refurbishing.

An area rug anchors these seating pieces, opposite, which have been pulled away from the walls.

FURNITURE FINESSE

Continue the fine old country tradition of finding fresh possibilities in familiar objects. Furniture doesn't have to be brand new. Something that is comfortably worn is often quite inviting. Wondering how to find new uses for what you already own? Here are a few things you can do.

smart steps

A mix-and-match assemblage of furniture, below, is unified by a pretty blue-and-white-print fabric.

one **Cover up, relocate, and recast.** Loose slipcovers and unusual throw pillows or casually tucked-in quilts can revive a has-been sofa, while a draping of chintz can hide an ugly end table. A tattered kitchen set becomes one-of-a-kind with a sponged or spatter-painted finish.

It seems simple, but just pulling the furniture away from the walls, arranging seating in a cozy grouping, or resettling a piece from another location can give a room a fresh aspect. Shine up the old dresser you've been hiding in the guest room, and move it into the entry hall. Stencil a set of tattered chairs that have been in the attic, and bring them down to brighten the breakfast room.

Sometimes clutter just needs a home to become something more. For instance, bound books scattered around the house or potted flowers make an impression when massed on shelves or a tabletop. Use a big old bowl to hold keys, change, and general junk.

two **Establish a focus.** Highlight the room's most dramatic features and support them with low-key elements. It's tempting to keep adding to a room, but the result can pull the

Formal upholstered high-back chairs, right, mix easily with an informal pine table in this appealing dining room.

Plain country furniture like this unassuming pine hutch, opposite, has traditionally been painted.

attention in too many directions. One or two focal points are usually all you need to anchor a room and give it drama.

three **Slow down.** Sometimes the first idea you have isn't the best solution. For example, after a move to a new home, you may want to settle everything immediately. But if you live with a room for a while, you can see how the light falls throughout the day, what looks best where, and in what areas people naturally congregate. Let your decorating plans evolve with your lifestyle.

But maintain balance in your caution. It's easy to talk yourself out of bold decorating strokes and into safe but sometimes uninteresting choices. Don't second-guess all the life out of your decorating decisions.

four **Aim for harmony spiced with a bit of variety.** Use the room's overall impression as the organizing principle. Does each addition advance the ambiance of the theme you envision? Dark tartan cushions would enhance an intimate masculine study, for example, but rough muslin curtains would not. However, some contrast or one element of surprise is often appealing—polished brass candlesticks lend just the right drama atop a rustic scrubbed pine table.

FURNITURE "STYLE"

In choosing furniture, you face a wide menu of traditional styles. America's earliest "Pilgrim" furniture often had a medieval flavor—straight legs and banister-like backs with lively turnings shaped on a lathe. In the mid-1700s, graceful Queen Anne chairs became fashionable, with their curvaceous cabriole legs and backs with carved center splats. This type of furniture overlapped with the heavily carved, robust Chippendale pieces that came into vogue during the second half of the eighteenth century and into the nineteenth century.

This mode was in turn eclipsed by the leaner, lighter, straighter Sheraton and Hepplewhite designs of the neoclassic Federal era, which thrived during the early nineteenth century. During the succeeding decades, furniture blossomed into a variety of exotic revival styles, most notably the heavily ornate furniture of high Victorian. The reaction to over-the-top Victorian design came with the bold straight-line forms of Craftsman furniture and the simple cottage pieces at the dawn of the twentieth century.

FURNITURE

When you're painting or refinishing furniture, don't forget to add the telling details, such as rustic reproduction hinges, elegant brass pulls, or whimsical painted ceramic knobs.

But such arbitrary style divisions often loosen up in country homes. Remember, many of the tables, chairs, benches, stools, and chests used by yesterday's farmers and workers were timeless, simple, and often homemade. Their economically straight, sturdy lines have been remarkably similar across the centuries. Just as in architecture, furniture of a particular style could persist in the country long after its fashionable reign. People rarely discarded anything, and country craftsmen tended to be conservative in adopting new designs. The latest mode might find interpretation in a simplified form or one that mixed freely with various elements of familiar styles. In essence, country furniture tended toward solid pieces, with nothing too fragile for daily life.

INFORMAL STYLES

Traditional vintage American furniture is noteworthy for its ingenuity—space-saving gateleg and drop-leaf tables, high-back settle benches, and spacious storage cupboards and chests. For example, on the westward expansion, a "food safe" or "jelly cupboard" might have been knocked together from packing crates to furnish a rough kitchen. Food tins decorated with hand-pierced designs often provided ventilated door panels for a pioneer's punched-tin food chests.

(In fact, personality-rich storage pieces can be vital to achieving a pleasing country room today. A well-chosen piece can conceal the modern accoutrements that often intrude on vintage-inspired surroundings.)

A prosperous rural house in centuries past might have acquired a few high-style pieces of furniture crafted in mahogany or walnut, frequently in veneers that revealed a wood's figured grain. Less costly country furniture in pine or maple was often painted or faux-grained to protect the wood and to make it more attractive. Today you can rely on the power of

paint in the same way to make inexpensive second-hand or unfinished furniture into distinctive pieces.

A PAIR OF COUNTRY FURNITURE FAVORITES

Two humble stars among America's country chairs are the Windsor chair and the rocker. Windsor chairs originated among English farmers: as they cleared back the encroaching woods, they gathered all the thin, flexible branches for stick furniture. Assembled of green or steam-softened wood, the pieces would shrink during drying, making them tight and sturdy. The back of a basic Windsor design has thin spindles that are enclosed by a hooped or straight rail above a solid seat. The chair's slightly splayed turned legs are strengthened by stretchers. In American

A rustic cross-brace bench, above, serves as a coffee table and counterpoint to the curvaceous camelback sofa.

An old cupboard, opposite, features pierced-tin doors originally intended for ventilation more than for decoration.

hands the Windsor proliferated in many forms, including a wide settee, a low-back "captain's chair," and a tall "comb-back" version with a curvy top rail.

From the 1700s onward, Americans in the city and the country valued Windsors for their lightness, modest price, and graceful durability. In an early example of mass production, apprentices would make and stockpile the components to keep the furniture makers busy with a salable staple product between custom commissions. To get the required strength, rigidity, or flexibility, these craftsmen combined different woods in each chair and usually painted them in rich colors, in keeping with the chairs' simple outlines. Furniture authority Wallace Nutting, writing in the 1930s, promoted an appreciation of Windsor chairs as "more suggestive of pleasant reflection than any other article of furniture."

The rocking chair's origins are misty, but by the 1700s it was another American favorite—this was a nation that liked motion, even when at leisure! Many early versions were simple standard chairs with the addition of rockers. But the notion soon engendered a variety of friendly styles.

- The slat-back, or ladder-back, rocker, popular from the 1700s to the late 1800s, when it was perfected by the Shakers
- A Boston, or Salem, rocker with a wide scooped seat, a spindle back, and a wide top rail, sometimes decoratively painted
- Windsor rockers, with spindle backs sometimes shaped for an "arrowback" profile
- Victorian wicker chairs; curvy, intricate, and light, with a summerhouse air
- Arts and Crafts or Mission rockers; massive and straight-lined, crafted in oak

Glider rockers might seem modern, but during the nineteenth century, at least a dozen patents set forth platform rockers with inventive arrangements of springs, straps, and pivots.

A rocking chair and a gateleg table, above, are examples of classic American furniture.

Windsor chairs, opposite, gathered around a trestle table, are perfect in a country dining room

Chapter Six

Upholstered pieces with
traditional styling, above,
are at home in a refined
country setting.

A checkered plaid fabric,
opposite, is always
appealing in a country
interior.

UPHOLSTERED PIECES

Our Colonial ancestors made simple wood furniture more comfortable with
cushions, perhaps brightened with "turkey work," a type of colorful dense
embroidery that suggested a Turkish rug. Early in the 1700s, houses of the well-to-
do featured the latest luxury: upholstered wing chairs with high enclosing backs to
shield drafts. The earliest examples are inventoried as bedroom furniture, often
reserved for the infirm. But by midcentury, such "easie chairs" and settees with
curved top lines and gently scrolled arms were company pieces, upholstered in
fine, solid-colored wools, embroidered flame-stitch fabrics, damasks, and florals.

Luckily in our own era, such soft nests are a standard part of everyday life. For the country spirit, sofas and chairs should be of generous proportions, in scale with the room, and usually of simple classic shapes.

- **Camelback** sofas have an eighteenth-century flavor. The curved back inspired the name. Characteristic of Hepplewhite and Chippendale styles, the camelback sofa can look more or less formal by the choice of fabrics.

- **Tuxedo** sofas feature a boxy frame that is typically associated with contemporary design. But you can soften this sofa's strong geometric lines with floral-print fabrics. If you choose a striped or plaid print, offset the angularity of the sofa's frame with a ruffled skirt and throw pillows.

- **Lawson** sofas, with rounded arms that are lower than the back, are classics and can present an invitingly plump form that looks at home in country settings, particularly when paired with a quaint country print.

A skirted sofa generally seems casual, while carved, exposed legs appear formal. However, pleated or tailored skirts can be formal as well. Sofas with loose pillows along the back need to be neatly arranged as a regular habit. Loose, informal covers can be a practical addition. Budget permitting, a seasonal change can be a charming notion, with pale linens and ticking for summer, and cozier wools and dark florals for winter.

Padded stools and ottomans invite you to put your feet up and relax, and their presence adds comfort and variety to a country room. They can serve for extra seating in a pinch and double as coffee tables or end tables.

COUNTRY FABRICS

Fabrics are the soul of decorating: sensual, soft, and evocative right down to their names—velvet, taffeta,

An eclectic country room, opposite, draws on varied textiles and textures to make it interesting.

chintz, paisley, muslin, *matelassé*. Country textiles encompass an intriguing range. From the seventeenth to the early nineteenth centuries, one of the basic chores in households was the spinning and weaving of rough homespun fabrics in wool, cotton, or the blended linen and wool of "linsey-woolsy." Often the yarns, tinted with home-brewed dyes, would be woven into simple contrasting stripes, checks, and plaids, staples of country decorating, whether in Scandinavia, France, or America. In later times, plain-woven cottons would be purchased and home-dyed. Thus you'll find that some simple, inexpensive fabric—plain wools, printed cottons, broadcloth, and rough unbleached muslins—create a warm, inviting effect in a country room.

SMART TIP

FINISHING TRIMS

Most country rooms are light on such details because they convey a certain grandeur. But carefully chosen details can add contrast or emphasize the graceful curve of a drape. To finish fabrics with a flourish, consider the array of fringes, tassels, cords, and decorative tapes. Fringes and tassels developed from the knots that tie the loose warp threads together to prevent unraveling. Making decorative tape and cord with small tabletop looms was a ladylike craft, and the results were put to use protecting seams and raw edges of curtains and upholstery.

THE INFLUENCE OF IMPORTED TEXTILES

Yesterday's homeowners also coveted finer, more-colorful fabrics, with names that betray their exotic origins: bright small-scale calico (named for Calicut, India); delicate gingham checks (from the Malay *genggang*, meaning "striped"); and glorious flower-decked chintzes (from the Hindi *chints*, for "bright spots"). From the seventeenth century onward, European producers slavishly imitated exports from Asia. France took the early lead, producing such distinctive eighteenth-century fabrics as the vivid Provençal cottons in small, repetitive prints, and toile de Jouy (named for the French city of Jouy), with finely etched scenic designs in blue or red on linen or cotton. An early country house might blend the utility fabrics of rough wools and home-tanned leather with a few treasured Old World fabrics, such as embroidered, large-scale crewelwork, some bits of velvet, or a brightly painted "tree of life" print from India.

Elegant eighteenth-century furniture demanded damasks, bold designs of Chinese influence, or rococo French swirls. After the American Revolution, sleek Sheraton and Hepplewhite pieces wore rich fabrics in plain colors, narrow stripes, rosettes, and Grecian motifs. French manufacturers even printed toiles with images of patriotic eagles and George Washington in a lion-drawn chariot.

Power looms for weaving, invented later in the eighteenth century, and the increasing ease of importing and transporting goods in the nineteenth century made fabrics of all kinds readily available, right down to the bright bolts of calico at the frontier general store. Honest utility fabrics, such as striped ticking made with a diagonal twilled weave for greater durability, flat-woven heavy sailcloth,

Floral-print fabrics in slightly faded tones lend a Victorian feeling to this cozy room, above.

Lace and needlepoint details enhance a romantic country interior, opposite.

and lightweight muslin in sturdy cotton, became workhorse choices. The Victorian era bloomed with floral prints, velvets, satins, and damask weaves.

SPECIAL FABRICS

A sense of tradition accompanies fabrics that suggest hard work. Embroidery's long history ranges from designs as bold as crewel in bright wool on rough linen

to finely shaded pictorial needlepoint. Pillows, chair seats, bed linens, and curtain edges and tiebacks offer small, bounded areas that can highlight such rich effects. Handcrafted textiles tend to be accents and are reviewed in the next chapter, "Country Details," beginning on page 110.

Lace is a most romantic textile, a froth of purely decorative impracticality. True handmade lace is created by two techniques.

● Needlepoint lace is stitched over a pattern drawn on fine linen, and the backing fabric is delicately cut away from the finished lacework.

● Bobbin, or pillow, lace is woven with long threads, weighted with hanging bobbins, and pinned over a pattern on a pillow. The lace maker deftly flips and twists the bobbins over and around each other, moving pins down as the knotted lace takes shape.

Similarly delicate openwork results from other widely practiced needlework techniques such as filet netting, knitting, tatting (a form of knotting made with a small shuttle), and crocheting, made popular by Irish immigrants. An 1854

Chapter Six

*In this spacious, many-windowed room, above,
soft yellow and mossy
green fabrics, white
wicker, and white
painted wood are all apt
to fade gracefully.*

needlework manual touted crochet as "one of those gentle means by which women are kept feminine and ladylike in this fast age." Despite such advantages, it was the era's machine-made products that made lace an affordable country finish for edging shelves and mantels or for trimming curtains and table linens. Antimacassars, lengths of lace laid on the arms and backs of sofas and chairs, defended the upholstery from the dark macassar hair oil used by nineteenth-century beaus. In the modern country room, lace is conveniently neutral in the color scheme, yet it has a refreshing lightness, whether with the sun shining through or as a pleasing contrast to dark wood.

CHOOSING FABRICS

Because fabric spans such variety, you can match a particular type to the job that makes the most of its qualities. For example, choose a tough linen blend for upholstery, a polished chintz for crisp pleated curtains, or a supple, translucent voile for a lushly draped window scarf. Woven designs generally bear up to more wear than printed fabrics, and midtone colors age more gracefully than very pale or dark fabrics.

The degree of formality is another guide. Informal fabrics are generally plain-woven in cotton or linen with bolder, simpler designs and a matte, homespun appearance. Sleek, understated fabrics with a silky or satiny texture have a delicacy that in small doses can add a pleasing contrast in a homey room.

Natural fibers are a logical choice to maintain a country mood. There are several basic choices.

- **Cotton** offers a good "hand" and durability, though it doesn't bear up to strong sunlight and is subject to staining unless treated or blended with synthetics.
- **Linen** is one of the most durable fibers. It often appears in mellow tones because it doesn't take dye well.
- **Wool** is sturdy and abrasion- and stain-resistant. It dyes beautifully but requires mothproofing.
- **Silk** is beautiful yet fragile and prone to fading.

Last, don't dismiss modern synthetics. Especially in blends with natural fibers, they can provide engineered advantages with a reasonably natural look and feel.

Country casual rooms appear to mix fabrics with abandon, but a few points will help them harmonize.

- Find links of similar texture and shared colors.
- Vary the scale. Two patterns of the same size can fight for attention.
- Look for simple mixers. Gentle geometric patterns, such as simple plaids, stripes, or checks, can make a harmonious coupling with each other or with florals. ✑

Antiques or Repros?

country decorators keep alive the instincts of our hunter-gatherer ancestors, spending happy days antiquing to find just the right piece. Along with the pleasures of the hunt, vintage items have the aura of age and authenticity that's one-of-a-kind. But for furnishing your daily life, don't overlook the benefits of a reproduction:

- Easy availability. Lacking the leisure to track down the perfect treasure, you may find it easier to deal with current inventories, available with just the colors and features you desire.
- The size of furniture pieces is scaled for today's taller people.
- A casual attitude. An antique, particularly a fine or fragile one, deserves respect, but it's okay to mix a few antiques with compatible new pieces.

7

COUNTRY DETAILS

Accessories and Collections

What often pulls together the lively, eclectic look of a country room are its delightful details and accessories. Finishing touches, personal possessions, and favorite things transform an impersonal space into an expressive and comfortable dwelling. Laura Ingalls Wilder, author of the Little House books, offers a perfect example of this when she describes how her family made over a rough frontier shanty and turned it into a real home, "with a blue bowl of grass flowers and windflowers on the table and a fashionable whatnot shelf where Ma's china shepherdess stood pink and white and smiling."

Accessories do more than decorate, however. They may serve practical functions, too. They certainly advance the design scheme by playing up the focal points or injecting bold colors or contrasting textures. But most often accessories exist to be admired, display workmanship, or convey a sense of history. Some add a dash of surprise, variety, and humor, especially because many charming country accessories began life as something else.

STARTING A COLLECTION

Sometimes the appreciation for the offbeat or handcrafted object turns into full-blown collecting. And for many homeowners, country decorating revolves around gathered treasures. Some craft pieces, baskets, or butter molds, for example, originally served utilitarian purposes. "Folk art" usually designates crafts such as portraits or carvings made strictly for decoration. But the line between the categories can be fuzzy.

Collecting often begins casually, with a few inherited pieces or objects picked up at tag sales or received as gifts. Some collections remain casual and expand with items that simply catch the owner's fancy. Other collections progress to a serious and sometimes scholarly pursuit of the rare, the old, and the unique. Here are some steps that might help shape your collecting philosophy.

smart steps

one **Buy items for your own satisfaction.** That's the standing advice of industry insiders. Speculative buying with hopes of selling again at a profit is always risky because of the fickleness of the hot collectible market. Look for your payback in your enjoyment of the object. Then if profit comes your way sometime in the future, think of it as gravy.

two **Find a category that fits your budget.** For example, certain varieties of turn-of-the-twentieth-century "art pottery" have become prohibitively expensive. Yet some whimsical ceramics from later decades may be more available and affordable. Within a given category, decide whether you'd rather take the time to save for a highly valuable item or be immediately gratified with a less rare or slightly damaged piece that's in your current price range.

three **Enjoy learning about your chosen collectible.** In our instant-communication age, it's easier than ever to develop relationships with other collectors and with specialized dealers through shows, newsletters, stores, and Web sites. Don't forget library and museum resources.

For most collectors, scouting flea markets, country auctions, shops, and shows is a pleasure in itself. Established dealers and auction houses provide as much information as possible in written form, including the piece's approximate age and perhaps its maker. Such "provenance" can add value to your purchase. Flea markets and garage sales may yield gems, but you're on your own, with no guarantees.

four **Learn about maintaining your collections.** If you're collecting delicate textile or paper pieces, find out what special care they need to preserve their integrity.

Recasting old things into new roles is a country custom. An old bedroom dresser, opposite, is pressed into service as a sideboard, and a stoneware pitcher serves as a generously proportioned vase for flowers.

A thoughtful display, below, focuses attention on textures and colors, even in workaday objects.

EVERYDAY ARTS

Authentic folk arts were passed down orally and through example within a limited audience familiar with the forms. The more isolated the group, the more distinctive the results. Some collectors enjoy exploring a range of crafts from a particular ethnic or regional group.

The Pennsylvania Dutch encompassed Germans, Swiss, Dutch, and Moravians in religious sects such as the Amish, Mennonites, and Dunkers. Their unique crafts include *scherenshnitte,* lacy, intricate designs skillfully snipped from paper, and *fraktur* documents in heavy Germanic calligraphy to commemorate births, baptisms, and weddings. *Fraktur* documents were embellished with stylized tulips, hearts, scrollwork, unicorns, and sun signs in bright, primary colors—symbols that reappear on the region's pottery, quilts, tinware, and painted furniture.

The Pennsylvania Dutch were only one of the many vigorous pockets of ethnic groups that influenced America's folk arts. Scandinavian settlers, concentrated in the Upper Midwest, produced finely carved utensils and richly painted chairs, cupboards, and dowry chests. Hispanics in the Southwest were noted for boldly carved furniture and small, finely detailed religious figures for household shrines. Folk historians are rediscovering veins of African influence in certain artifacts of basketry, musical instruments, quilts, ceramics, and wood sculpture.

But distinctive folk art isn't limited to specific ethnic groups. A subculture such as whalers, isolated on long voyages, would arrive home with striking examples of "scrimshaw" made of whale bones and teeth, carved and incised with fine-lined sketches to make corset stays, pie crimpers, birdcages, clothespins, toys, walking sticks, and sculptures.

Almost anything can become a collectible—from furniture and tableware to hatpins, buttons, and spoons. A die-hard collector is happiest when finding treasure amid the "trash." But a few broad categories are favored by collectors.

Time-worn shades of blue, above, link a bevy of antique trays, boxes, and buckets.

Colorful ceramics, opposite, present a united front of bright, simple outlines.

QUICK TIP

ACCESSORIES

Turn necessary storage into an accessory.
The painted umbrella stand in the foyer, the basket
of napkins on the table, ribbon-tied candles on the
sideboard, and a carved-leather box for bills
are ideas for decoratively
corralling clutter.

Blue and white are traditional colors that nicely tie together this array of sturdy spongeware bowls and pitchers, above left.

A collection of valuable antique toys, above right, adds a wistful note of nostalgia to a faithful nineteenth century-style country home.

CERAMICS

One of humanity's oldest crafts, ceramics has evolved over the centuries into a delightful assortment of objects, ranging from wrought porcelain figurines to chunky everyday pottery. All types of ceramics have their enthusiasts.

In the seventeenth and eighteenth centuries, American colonists coveted Europe's colorful glazed majolica, China's blue-and-white export porcelains, and Dutch and English blue-and-white transferware that imitated the Chinese products. From their native iron-rich clays, Early Americans produced low-fired red-earthenware pottery, often decorated with "slip," or liquefied clay. Slip could be "trailed" on in decorative patterns or coated on the piece and selectively etched away for a *sgraffito* (scratched) design. Mochaware, another nineteenth-century earthenware, features swirling patterns produced with drips of colored acid on the wet slip.

As kilns improved, high-fired, less porous stoneware became more common, often finished with "salt glazing" techniques brought by German immigrants.

From the eighteenth century onward, ceramics poured out of factories in the Potteries District of Staffordshire, England. Some of it was exceedingly elegant.

But many of today's country collectors seek out the utilitarian pieces, such as ironstone, a heavy and simple white china with iron slag mixed into the clay. It was imported by the ton for America's everyday use.

From the late nineteenth century through the Depression, America's idiosyncratic "art potteries" each produced their own distinctive range of products. These pieces are now eagerly hunted down, whether a lustrously glazed Rookwood vase or a lively cookie jar from Ohio's McCoy Pottery.

Some ceramics lovers zero in on a particular manufacturer or variety, while others focus on a certain category, developing a mania for teapots, cup-and-saucer sets, commemorative plates, or salt-and-pepper shakers, to name just a few.

BASKETS

Weaving is another ancient craft. Native Americans were skilled basket makers, and each group of immigrants brought its own weaving traditions, such as the fragrant sea-grass baskets from Gullah Islands off the Carolinas, which derive from African inspirations. Even sailors on whaling ships made baskets.

The raw materials can be flexible reeds, tropical rattan palms, ferns, grasses, or flat wood splints to make a particularly sturdy, if usually expensive, hardwood basket. A basket's form follows its function. For example, market baskets are large and flat-bottomed for generous carrying capacity. Wall baskets are flattened on the back to hang neatly on a hook. Vegetable baskets are big and coarsely woven to allow air to circulate. Berry baskets are smooth and fine to avoid poking or dropping delicate fruits.

An open caddy, above, stores a basket collection as a display of textures, accented by a woven wall hanging.

TOYS

Well-loved and well-used playthings are popular collectibles, probably for their happy associations. Dolls are an endless category. Nineteenth-century doll makers experimented with papier mâché, new rubber compounds, and glazed and unglazed ceramics to achieve lifelike effects. By the early 1900s, "baby" dolls had become more popular than "lady" dolls, and such favorite American character dolls as the Kewpie and Raggedy Ann came into being. Preprinted cloth dolls, to be cut, stitched, and stuffed, and more rustic homemade rag and cornhusk dolls were simpler country versions. Teddy bears, introduced during Theodore Roosevelt's presidency and named for him, still have a strong coterie of admirers.

Victorian game boards and country checkerboards, with their simple painted designs, are valued as eye-catching wall art.

HOUSEHOLD TEXTILES

In earlier times, needlework was part of a well-bred woman's

education. Fancy stitchery was taught in the best girls' schools, but everyone learned basic dressmaking, mending stitches, and some simple embroidery. What these efforts left behind are the samplers used to practice these skills. Whether simple or elegantly wrought, these stitched panels still exude sincerity. Less common, but still attractive, are samplers of knitting and crochet stitches.

Beyond the classic country quilt, eighteenth- and nineteenth-century woven coverlets are another example of history-rich bedding. Woven first by housewives, then more intricately by itinerant weavers with Jacquard looms, the two-tone reversible coverlets tell a story in words that were stitched in red and indigo blue against a natural tan background.

Some collectors seek the Old World grace of antique lace and tablecloths. For a livelier look, consider the vintage kitchen linens of the 1930s and '40s, with their playful patterns of teacups, puppies, or flowers, in rich primary colors.

GLASS

Fragile glass always seems precious. That's obvious in the case of glittering cut-crystal de-canters and goblets. But even humble cast-off bottles from the early days of manufacturing seem to be lucky survivors, avidly sought by collectors. In the late nineteenth and early twentieth centuries, art glass workshops produced exquisite pieces, such as the luminously colorful Tiffany vases still pursued by enthusiasts with deep pockets.

But it was also an era when new manufacturing technology made

Vintage needlework on stacks of pillows, opposite, harks back to a time when such decorative flourishes were always made by hand.

Glassware should be displayed to catch the light. In these etched and pressed pieces, below, the illumination enhances the delicate clear and matte patterns

glass an everyday object. Less-prestigious products such as "carnival glass," made iridescent with metal oxides sprayed onto the molten surface, and "Depression glass," with its low-relief pressed or etched designs and soft, mellow colors, have become collectibles in their own right.

IN THE EYE OF THE BEHOLDER

In earlier centuries, traveling sign painters and decorative painters peddled their skills from village to village. These self-trained artists were equally happy to undertake a portrait or a landscape for a willing customer. The resulting paintings often have a directness and detail irresistible to the collector. If genuine antique country paintings are too expensive to pursue, consider modern reproductions that can carefully evoke the straightforward style of the originals.

Vintage Advertising Art. By its nature, vintage advertising art makes an immediate connection with viewers, using bright, bold graphics somewhat weathered by time. Tins, painted signs, boxes, advertisements, and promotional items from the early days of packaged goods radiate a naive, nostalgic earnestness.

WOOD AND METAL CRAFTS

Skillful hands once turned readily available wood into monumental artworks such as ship figureheads, trade signs, cigar-store Indians, and carousel horses. But many collectors seek out smaller crafts: whittled figures, the chipped-wood frames of "tramp art," boxes decoratively etched with wood-burning pokers, or skillfully painted duck decoys.

Gleaming silver has for centuries been the most coveted tableware. By the mid-1700s, America's own silvermaking was of the highest order, often in simple, classic designs that are still reproduced.

Country-minded collectors also enjoy humbler metalware, such as pewter, originally a tin or lead alloy with a soft, silvery luster once used in modest households across Europe and America. Genuinely old pewter is rather rare because people customarily traded it in when they purchased new pieces. But many manufacturers now reproduce the bold, simple housewares of earlier times or intricate figurines in today's lead-free pewter. So unless you must have the genuine article, consider a faithful, accessible, and affordable lookalike.

Even humble, utilitarian metal cookware, such as old tin cooking pots or porcelain-enameled graniteware from the nineteenth century, have their fans. A more decorative household metal, from the eighteenth century onward, is "tole." This tin plate was and is still used for trays, plates, lamp shades, and decorative objects. It's distinguished by its designs of flowers, birds, and fruit painted on a black background to make the colors glow.

DISPLAYING A COLLECTION

Of course, one of the most gratifying aspects of collecting is displaying your wares. However, there is an art to creating a pleasing arrangement of objects, particularly if they are dissimilar in size and shape. If you plan to showcase

Flat, bright folk-art painting provided the stylistic inspiration for a pair of French farmyard scenes, above left.

Vintage housewares, above right, create an evocative vignette on a rugged hutch.

Old-fashioned advertising art, such as this poster of a satisfied cigar smoker, opposite, catches the eye and sparkles with personality.

your collection of treasures or even display just a few favorite things, these steps will help to shape your presentation.

smart steps

one   **Look for links.** Group items with a shared element, whether by theme, material, shape, or design. The link could be dogs rendered in ceramic, embroidery, or paint; sugar-and-creamer sets from Colonial silver to Depression glass; a blue glass goblet juxtaposed with patent-medicine bottles; or family pictures that are all in round frames.

Consider also how the items relate to their location in terms of viewing distance and theme. Is it a nicely detailed piece that should be appreciated close-up (maybe under glass) or a simple, colorful object that would catch the eye if placed high on a tall shelf? Old tinware makes a logical display in a breakfast area, and children's books look at home in a reading corner.

two   **Distinguish between storage and display.** If you've amassed a significant collection, decide whether all of it has to be on view. Sometimes several smaller organized presentations are more effective. In a collection of teacups, for example, singling out just the bright floral ones or the blue-and-white wares could make a stronger display. Some collectors enjoy rotating their treasures so that the collection always appears fresh.

three   **Group together small objects.** Do this for visual impact. With imagination, almost anything can make an attractive

display: seashells heaped in glass bowls, vintage postcards tacked on a piece of trellis, belt buckles or buttons mounted on black velvet. Old drawers for printer's type, with their tiny partitions, are a favorite display aid.

four **Define the display.** Decide whether you want to suggest abundance or prefer to spotlight a few special items. Old toys might look especially fun and spirited in a slightly random, over-the-top presentation. Conversely, isolating a few fine pieces of heirloom silver encourages examination of their intricate details.

five **Look for unexpected display spots.** A curving staircase can hold a few decorative objects outside the railing or on a wide landing outside the traffic aisle. A long, low bench in a wide hallway or a shelf recessed into the stud

Collected items also gain resonance from a shared theme. This mantel grouping, above, takes on added charm with its subtle overtones of seagoing adventures.

Groupings have maximum impact. Arranged on a side table covered in a country-checked cloth, opposite, a collection of old stove-heated irons takes on a sculptural character.

space on a short wall can show off small items. You can also effectively display items in bay windows or even on a windowsill as long as they don't get in the way. Pick a spot that shows the collection to advantage, such as a sunny window shelf for glassware or a low table for textural wood pieces that encourage onlookers to touch.

six **Gear displays to your lifestyle.** Don't expand a stash of dustables unless you can keep them under glass. If you've already collected a few active toddlers and a tail-wagging dog, nix a coffee table porcelain display—everyone will be happier with the breakables in glass-fronted cupboards or high up on valance shelves.

HORIZONTAL DISPLAYS

Open shelves and display furniture, such as hutches or glass-fronted display vitrines, provide a natural framework and are easy places to gather items. Too easy, in fact: they invite you to keep adding pieces, creating clutter instead of a coherent presentation.

Completely symmetrical arrangements, such as a mantelpiece clock and two flanking candlesticks, generally set a calm, formal mood. A casual asymmetrical arrangement takes trial and error, for it should still seem balanced and in scale. Place the larger items first, and then offset their visual weight with groups of smaller items. Experiment with varying heights, colors, and textures, such as playing off gleaming glass against rough stone. Give a fine sculptural or brightly detailed piece enough space for proper appreciation.

Tablescapes. Because tables tend to be clutter catchers, a display on one should appear as a composed still life. Of course, you can't use the dinner table. But even

COUNTRY FLOWERS

For instant, uncomplicated charm, it's hard to compete with flowers. Country rooms tend to feature simple, familiar blooms, such as daffodils, roses, pansies, or geraniums, or branches cut from flowering lilacs and forsythia. Whether you're displaying flowers in lush armloads or as a few delicate blooms, take time to find an unexpected bowl or pot to set off the display.

on a table that doesn't get much use, you must still leave enough room around the display for daily needs—a spot to place a cup on the coffee table or the keys on the front hall's sideboard.

WALL DISPLAYS

Quilts, tapestries, rugs, or major artworks may be large enough to hang on the wall in isolation. Such standouts are usually placed to be visible from the doorway. Many smaller items, however, look best above an anchoring piece of furniture, to which they should bear a graceful relationship—large artwork over a spindly side table looks top-heavy, while a small sketch will appear lost above a sofa. Artwork should hang at eye level, taking into account whether viewers will be sitting or standing. When in doubt, hang pieces lower rather than higher; artwork that is too high can seem to "float."

A grouping of framed wall art should share a color or unifying theme. Similar frames and mat colors might pull together a really diverse group. But as long as some organizing link exists, a mixed composition can have a friendly country looseness. Wall art can extend beyond paintings to posters, maps, plates, memorabilia, sheet music, invitations, or anything else you can attractively mount and frame.

A picket-fence window screen, opposite, *pulls together a loosely composed tabletop display.*

A symmetrical composition, below, *plays up the serenity of rugged bits of nature and art.*

DRIED DISPLAYS

Most well-run farm
households customarily had
a small garden for
herbs, which were used for
cooking and curing.
Families passed down
not just recipes
for remedies and fragrant
combinations but information
on harvesting, drying,
and preserving these herbs.
For today's home,
a little of that history
can be brought back with
crafts using natural
dried materials, such as
fragrant potpourris and
casually knotted wreaths
and garlands.

To devise a graceful composition for several pieces of wall art, decide on an overall shape for the grouping: circle, square, rectangle, or triangle. With masking tape, mark out the proposed framework on the floor. Lay down the artwork and experiment, placing the larger items first and balancing them with smaller pieces of artwork, moving the masking tape as needed. When you're satisfied, tape the same "framework" on the wall and re-create the arrangement.

Family photos are the most personal of accessories, full of history and tradition. An appealing frame, perhaps one that is handmade, may be inartistic, but it can make a sentimental family photo more pleasing. An antique frame (or a faithful reproduction) can add a vintage look. To give visual weight to a small photo, set it off with a wide mat. Choose a frame to complement the picture: some pictures can carry off an ornate frame; others call for understatement. 🖎

A charming, grayed corner closet, opposite, becomes a lovely backdrop for a dried flower arrangement and naturally woven wreath.

For a desk corner, below, an assortment of vintage prints has a personal, lively aspect. Yet the artwork is unified by using similiar frames and is contained in a neat, rectilinear outline.

Quintessentially Country Quilts

if country decorating has one symbol, it's most likely the quilt. While rooted in several European traditions, this craft flowered in the United States, where it still thrives. For display, sturdy quilts can be draped casually over furniture or hung on racks and refolded periodically to even out the wear. More fragile quilts, hung on a wall, may need to be supported at all four sides. Pieces from damaged, not-too-valuable quilts can be made into pillows, or they can be folded and stacked to play off each other's patterns and colors. All fabric artwork should be kept from damaging direct sunlight.

Framed prints, left, can be grouped by theme for visual impact.

8

THE COLORS OF
COUNTRY
From Nature's Palette

Color, like music, evokes a mood. And for achieving

a country atmosphere, whether of a cozy cottage,

a rugged farmhouse, or a rumpled manor, color is

a powerful tool. But choosing the right color can be

confusing in today's world of so many possibilities. That's

a new quandary. Throughout most of history, people were

limited to locally available colors and influenced by regional

climate and customs. Thus deep historical associations are

embodied in specific palettes—the earthy hues of

a Tuscan villa, the sober tones of a New England keeping

room, the strong reds of the Spanish-influenced Southwest.

REAL COLOR

Most country palettes incline toward the mellow side, reflecting the natural tones of wood and stone and the softer tints rendered with vegetable dyes and earth colors. Museum researchers microanalyzing paints in Colonial rooms have determined that although the more somber colors of the past have come down to us in fairly true form, what was once a bright Prussian blue may have darkened to a pine green, or a lively verdigris to a muddy brown.

Prior to the paints and dyes of modern chemistry, vivid hues tended to be "fugitive" and subject to fading and softening. Visitors to restored historic houses are sometimes startled by the intense colors our forebears reserved for their best rooms. In earlier times, bright colors were expensive and prized, and modest households would use such touches sparingly. An embroidery sampler showing off a daughter's skill, a painted chest to hold linens, or treasured pieces of pottery, with their fired-on color, would be given a special place.

But with today's infinite range of color choices, how do you start narrowing the field into a workable color scheme? Try these steps.

smart steps

one **Consider historical roots.** If your house has a decided architectural character or you're drawn to a particular period, find inspiration in researching the era's typical colors. The British-influenced Colonial palette—grayed

blues and greens, dun yellows, yellowish greens, and earthy "cupboard" reds—
lingered long in rural settings. During the nineteenth century, with new
chemical dyes, premixed paints, and mechanized printing, colorful fabrics and
wallpapers became more commonplace in middle-class houses, sometimes in
garishly bright combinations.

two   **Determine the practical demands on your color scheme.** Do the
new additions need to mesh with existing collections or furnishings? Is housekeeping a big issue? Then steer clear of white and bright surfaces, and incline

*This living room's neu-
tral, natural hues, above,
emphasize the rugged
textures of stone, wicker,
plaster, and wood.*

*Country colors tend
toward the mellow, as
in this kitchen corner's
medley of soft, smoky
blues and tans, opposite.
Strong yellow contrasts
add some spark.*

Color choices can play with our perceptions of space. In this dining room, below, pale yellow walls visually expand the space and give a glow to the natural light.

toward dirt-hiding midtones and neutrals. Are you looking for low-key, livable colors for a much-used room? Or a more exuberant country atmosphere? Do you want to spotlight your fine furniture against a pale, understated background? Or do you want to "fill" a sparsely furnished room with several rich background colors and visual textures?

three **Consider the room's size and natural light.** In general, light colors make a room seem larger. But that needn't determine your choice. Better a room that seems a tad smaller, yet lively and welcoming with color.

Warm a dark, north-facing space with soft pinks, beiges, and golds. Or if a room bakes in the afternoon sun, temper it with cool blues and violets.

four **Don't hesitate to play favorites.** Using too many colors in your scheme can confuse the eye. Organize the room by letting one color dominate and give the room its flavor. A favorite color can even be the basis for a monochromatic color scheme, which plays a single hue out in its different tints, shades, and tones. This single-minded approach might seem too staged for an easygoing country room, though, unless it's loosened up with neutrals and naturals.

five **Try out the possibilities.** It's hard to visualize how colors can affect each other until you get some real-life samples. Bring the proposed ingredients together, and live with them for a few days. Look at the lineup both in natural and artificial light before making your decision.

THINKING ABOUT COLORS

The Color Wheel

Designers use the color wheel, which is pictured on this page, to think abstractly about color choices. This design tool portrays the spectrum of pigment colors as a circle with red, blue, and yellow at equidistant points. These are the primary colors, which can't be made by combining other colors; in between are the colors created when the primaries are combined in changing proportions. Though often neatly diagrammed as a series of discrete pie slices, the color wheel is actually a continuum, as one color gradually mixes toward the next in imperceptible steps. The wheel as a whole divides loosely between warm reds and yellows, and cool greens and blues. The color wheel's pure, vivid saturated hues are generally used in small doses, particularly in a gentle-spirited country room. These hues can be lightened with white into progressively lighter tints, darkened with black into progressively deeper shades, or mellowed with gray into dustier tones. These less intense versions predominate in interiors because they're livable when used in quantity.

Analogous Colors

COMPLEMENTARY AND ANALOGOUS COLORS

Directly opposite any hue on the color wheel is its strongest possible contrast, known as its complement. High-contrast pairings in a complementary color scheme tend to enhance each other and make for a lively, energetic setting. While blue and orange might sound a bit gaudy, remember that each color represents a range, and the pair could be rendered as cobalt blue and terra-cotta, or stone blue and bittersweet. In complementary schemes, one color is usually center stage, while the other serves as the sharpening accent.

Neighboring colors on the wheel share a common ground that tends to make them harmonious when used together in an analogous color scheme. A primary color will often harmonize with a range of colors that lie alongside it—for example, a red playing off one of the reddish orange tints. Adding in a color from the other side of the same primary (in this example, where red turns toward purple) could potentially be more discordant—or merely lively, depending on the exact choices and the quantities.

Complementary Colors

Determining which colors coordinate with each other is hardly a rule-bound science—the decision usually requires some trial and error with real-life samples. Painstakingly matched colors can sometimes seem a bit contrived for a relaxed country room. For a looser approach, think of chosen colors as a range of possibilities, and seek harmony rather than a perfect match.

COLOR FAMILIES

Blue is a favorite country color, with suggestions of steadfast reliability and calm reflection. Its association with sky and sea lends a cool, retreatlike quality that's refreshing and space enhancing.

Some of the earliest dyes derived from the European herb woad and its more potent tropical cousin, indigo. Both produced the cool, deep blue used in such staple country fabrics as twilled ticking stripes, denim, and the stripes and checks of homespun fabrics. Colonial woodwork was sometimes painted a deep gray-blue or green-blue, while classically oriented Federal-era rooms turned toward airier skylike tints. Blue has a long tradition in ceramics, from the clear, intense cobalt blue of Chinese import porcelain and Dutch and English delftware to the misty blue of Wedgwood.

The color blue connotes harmony and serenity, but it also has endless moods from delicate to bold. Everyone has a favorite blue.

The color red is exhuber-ant and versatile. Red glows by sunlight, espe-cially during the after-noon. It's flattered by incandescent light, too.

The color remains true across a wide tonal range, whether it's crisp navy, bright azure, or a tender baby blue. All of them are compatible with one another. Blue also stands up to strong contrasts, such as clear white or a softer cream. It mixes well with yellow of equal intensity, as in the vivid blues and egg-yolk yellows of tightly patterned French country fabrics or the rich stone blue and cream of Swedish settings. When you're decorating, remember that dark blues can seem formal, while rustic blues, grayed down toward stonelike tints, appear easygoing. Grayed blues often demand a bright accent color, such as bandanna red.

Red has always been loved for its attention-grabbing energy, whether in the red hearts and tulips of Pennsylvania Dutch embroidery, in the swirling rosemaling painting of Norwegian country hope chests, or in coveted bits of imported calicos, dyed with madder plants. For its reputed ability to gather the sun's warmth, red is also the traditional color for barns.

At its boldest, pure scarlet red is generally reserved for accents. Many country reds are instead slightly weathered and softened. From antiquity onward, walls have been washed with red ocher mineral pigments for an earthy russet color. Darkened to bricklike tones, red can become almost a vigorous neutral. Red seems more sophisticated in clear, dark shades of wine and maroon, but never loses that vitality that makes it a favorite in lively family rooms and hospitable

SMART TIP

COLOR SCHEMES

A time-proven method is to start with a print you love and use it lavishly. From the print, choose a light tint to use for the background color, a midtone for some large furniture elements, and the strongest hues for the "top notes" of the accents. Be sure to add some neutrals and intriguing textures to keep the whole scheme from looking matched or contrived.

The color yellow is lumi-nous and lighthearted. Soft yellow can be an unobtrusive backdrop, but a strong shade may be overpowering.

dining rooms. It's more delicate and romantic in its lighter tints of floral pink, which simply hint at red's warmth without its assertiveness.

Yellow is the most luminous of colors, and therefore the most eye-catching. It always seems full of sunshine, and as a countermeasure to gray days, yellow appears in soft buttery tones in Swedish country rooms or in buttercup hues in English cottages. Clear yellows seem sharper and livelier when made more "acid" with a touch of green.

Used at full strength, yellow can jump at the viewer and disrupt a color scheme. But in soft tints of cream and straw, it's eminently mixable. Yellow isn't a dense color and quickly takes a green or brown cast when darkened. The subdued tones of

mustard, buff, and olive-yellow make yellow's glow more earthbound. These undemanding yellows are time-honored in country settings, even if just for a few yellowware bowls used for accents. Because yellow is so responsive to the light, be sure that your choice looks as inviting by artificial illumination as by sunlight.

Green is not a primary color but a mixture of blue and yellow. However, most people consider green a basic color, and with its mix of warm and cool, a particularly refreshing, balanced hue. Symbolic of life and growth, green is nature's favorite color and can vary from the tender yellow-greens of a new leaf to the bright green of grass, to the darkness of shadowy firs. In general, true greens and those inclining toward blue are cool and space enhancing. Soft sage and yellow tints can be quite warm and earthy. Though bright apple greens were fashionable in the late 1700s and a "greenery-yallery" was a popular Arts and Crafts color, some greens in that family might seem too acid and sharply modern for a mellow country scheme.

NEUTRALS AND NATURALS

These "no-color" colors include black, white, and gray; the whole appealing range of off-whites, beiges, and browns; and the

The color green is natural and revitalizing. As in nature, greens can be mixed freely, but be careful: blue-greens may clash with yellow-greens in equal quantities.

You won't find neutrals (white, black, and brown) on the color wheel, but these mix-ables play an important role in decorating.

inherent tones of wood, stone, and metal. Neutrals have practical advantages: they are agreeable mixers, good choices for long-term investments, and in darker versions, fairly forgiving of everyday wear. For a country room, neutrals are easygoing choices that can embody an unpretentious, "undecorated" naturalness. When color is down-played, the focus is on texture, which can give a room a rugged, tactile appeal.

Neutrals include white, black, and brown. White has a freshness and simplicity, and can be crisp and cool or dainty as lace. But it can seem sterile as an overall scheme unless you give it warm textural interest or some touches of color, which glow even brighter with a white contrast.

Black, strong and dramatic, has long punctuated country rooms, whether in wrought-iron hardware, black-painted Hitchcock chairs, or the crisp black-and-white checks of a painted floorcloth.

Brown, produced by varying amounts of yellow, red, and black, is easily produced using earth pigments and a variety of organic dyes. As such, it carries connotations of sturdy homeyness. Its considerable range runs from soft tints to toasty midtones to almost-black umber. Brown also encompasses the tones of natural leathers and woods' varied hues, from ebony to yellow pine. Deep browns are best with bright accents and light contrasts to keep them cozy. 🐪

9

IN THE KITCHEN
With Country in Mind

Americans have always combined comfortable traditions with current inventiveness in the kitchen. Country colors, finishes, and patterns seem especially right here. As the busiest room in the house, the kitchen serves many daily needs. But it also carries symbolic weight as the place where we share work and food among familiar things and friendly faces. It's the room that most clearly says "home."

The earliest settlers recalled the kitchens of their native countries. The English colonists created rooms that glowed with wood paneling, which they painted

*Rough antique wooden-
wares,* opposite top,
*lend a kitchen a timeless
simplicity.*

*A reclaimed functional
antique stove,* opposite
bottom, *is a lavish
historic accent.*

*By the glow of vintage-style
lamps,* below, *a country
kitchen functions smoothly
with its generous marble-
topped worktable.*

rich red, grayed teal, and deep green. German and Dutch colonists in the New
World tended toward bright colors, with high-contrast decorative painting.

AN EVOLVING STYLE

The earliest American kitchens focused on a wide fireplace. While we romantically
picture a roaring fire, a skilled open-hearth cook would manage her fuel carefully,
often scooping a hot pile of coals out onto the brick hearth floor to make a separate "burner." For the weekly baking, she might fire up the back oven, which was
built into the fireplace wall.

   Hot, laborious open-hearth cooking inspired many ingenious devices: revolving
toasters, waffle irons, long-handled "spider" skillets, and Dutch ovens, with

flanged lids to hold coals scooped on top. Early Americans used a ratchet to raise and lower the large cooking pots that slow-simmered meat. Crude reflector ovens held meat on a revolving spit until it was "done to a turn." While metalwares were treasured purchases, most cooks also had a supply of homemade "treen," or wooden spoons, cups, and ladles, made by any handy whittler. Such simple early kitchenwares are evocative collectibles today.

In the mid-1800s, only the romanticists sighed over the demise of open-hearth cooking, as households quickly embraced the cast-iron cookstove that burned wood or coal. A prototype gas range appeared at the Great Exhibition of 1851 in London and at the first electric kitchen at the 1893 Chicago World's Fair. But it was well into the 1930s before these appliances came home. At that time, refrigerators arrived and by the late 1940s were considered as fundamental as the modern range and running water.

MODERN KITCHEN CHARM

The purist, with a sufficient budget, can convincingly conceal modern appliances with specialized cabinetry. Dishwashers, microwaves, trash compactors, and refrigerators can disappear completely behind cabinet doors, perhaps with some decorative fretwork for ventilation. Some new and expensive refrigerators and freezers are modular and are installed much like drawers in various work zones instead of standing as one large unit. Dishwashers, too, are available as compact modular units. In a large kitchen, you can locate one near the main sink and another near a secondary bar or island sink.

For less rigorous disguise, matching-panel fronts on the major appliances help blend them into the cabinetry. Appliances can even be concealed with a colorful, washable curtain attached to the counter's overhang. In a colorful kitchen, appliances painted at a local auto body shop in sky blue or geranium red can become whimsical additions. Or apply a stenciled design or a faux finish to appliance fronts. Several manufacturers also offer modern gas and electric ranges styled like

Earthy floor tiles and painted finishes in weathered midtones, above, make an efficiently fitted kitchen seem more mellow.

Open shelves and a hutch join freestanding appliances, opposite, in a country kitchen.

old wood-burning stoves. But to contemporary eyes, standard appliances tend to be unobtrusive. If your kitchen is rich with colors, textures, and collectibles, most observers will skim over the appliances as expected background. Appliances in standard, simple designs work best for this strategy.

THE "UNFITTED" LOOK

The informal family kitchen wasn't designed but evolved along functional lines. Individual pieces of furniture—a table, a cupboard, shelves, a hutch, or an armoire, sometimes retired from the finer "company" rooms—were added as needed. This loose, unfitted look is a hallmark of a humble country kitchen.

Amid the current design-world hoopla about the "return of the unfitted kitchen," look critically at such plans, particularly if you're an enthusiastic cook. While unfitted designs can provide a handsome country look, they may lack the workspace or convenient configurations that make a room a pleasure to work in.

Many country enthusiasts find a middle ground in loosening up modern kitchen planning with selected, character-rich pieces and accessories, open shelving, and eye-catching finishes. A spacious floor plan allows leeway for idiosyncratic touches. In a large kitchen, an island styled differently from the wall cabinets or even a big farmhouse table with baskets underneath will add usable workspace with a casual, random look.

STORAGE STRATEGIES

Many kitchen renovations spring from a lack of storage space, as appliances and ingredients proliferate and strain the capacity. When you're decorating, remember that while a down-home kitchen may charmingly suggest endless bounty, bulging clutter is less appealing. There are some steps you can take to ensure efficient storage in a country kitchen.

smart steps

one **Zero in on necessities.** Before declaring your storage inadequate, make sure that every item is pulling its weight. If you use the fish poacher, cake decorator, and turkey platter twice a year, store them elsewhere. Watch out for

Open storage nooks in this island, opposite, capitalize on the appeal of serving ware. Items stored this way should be ones used and washed often because they are a catchall for grease and grime.

Kitchen staples, below, can be presented decoratively as demonstrated by rows of spices in an old apothecary shelf.

needless duplication. Don't give prime storage to dozens of glasses or stacks of mixing bowls when you typically use only a few.

two **Plan point-of-use storage.** Put the baking spices within reach of the mixer and the savory spices near the stove. Targeting storage may even free up room for other things such as baskets, tins, or an extra freestanding corner cabinet or work cart.

three **Let practical wares double as decoration.** The yellowed plastic spatulas can stay in the drawer, but wooden spoons, the old sifter, canisters, skeins of herbs or garlic, or earthenware bowls can all give a room a friendly bustle while providing a useful function.

four **Use open storage strategically.** It makes sense to reserve open storage for items that you use frequently. That way they don't just gather grimy dust. Be wary of the hanging pot rack directly over the cooktop, where pots can quickly get grubby from spattering grease and liquids.

CABINETRY

Cabinetry usually costs more than any other item in a kitchen renovation, and it has the biggest impact on the room's style. Before junking existing cabinets, consider whether refinishing, perhaps with a personality-rich faux effect, or refacing with new doors can reclaim basically sound units.

Today's cabinets run a gamut of country styles: rustic planked fronts, more formal cathedral-arched panels, or classic square panels, recessed or raised. The range of woods to choose from is equally wide. Oak, with its rugged grain, is the most popular, adaptable choice.

Kitchen cabinet fashions oscillate between very light and very dark stain treatments, so a midtone

get dated in just a few short years.

If you incline toward dark, cozy woods, make sure the kitchen is well lit, and keep other elements on the light side. White-enameled cabinetry can have a cottage-fresh appeal but will require some upkeep. Among bolder choices is a color-stain or a painted finish in a Shaker blue or Nantucket green, perhaps with a distressed or antiqued finish, for example. Stenciling or freehand painting can add still more individuality to cabinet fronts, but only if you do it sparingly.

Glass-fronted cabinets and open shelves break up the mono-lithic banks of cabinetry while showing off the wares inside. But don't install them if you can't make a pleasing arrangement of the contents and keep them neat.

COUNTER FORCES

Counters can be great places for showcasing interesting collections. But unless you've got a spacious kitchen, it's more practical to keep counters clutter-free and reserve these surfaces for work. Place countertop and hand-held appliances in a convenient location where they'll be easy to retrieve, perhaps in a corner storage garage. A swing-up tray for a heavy stand mixer is a nice luxury, but it will consume considerable interior cabinet space.

Plastic Laminate. In a country kitchen, countertop materials should appear natural or, barring that, unobtrusive. Plastic laminate is reasonably priced and is easy to install or replace. High-quality plastic laminate is durable, though prone to chipping that can't be repaired, scorching, and water-infiltration at sink-side seams. More expensive solid-core laminates eliminate the dark joints and offer fancy multihued edge treatments. But in a country setting, laminates are perhaps best presented in low-key, unfussy forms, in simple neutral colors.

Solid-Surfacing Material. The same applies to solid-surfacing material, a synthetic made from polyester or acrylic, sometimes mixed with ground stone. It generally costs three to five times as much as standard plastic laminate but is

Glass doors break up massive cabinetry, above. Save them for where you want to display pretty contents.

Homey slat-fronted cabinets in a buttery finish, opposite, embody a straightforward charm.

hard-wearing, repairable, and good-looking. It's offered now in a rainbow of choices and faux looks, including some convincing stone impressions. Skilled professional installers can create decorative inlay effects.

Wood. Wood has natural country warmth, but as a countertop is subject to water damage and warping. You may want to limit wood to a chopping surface. Durable eastern sugar maple is common for laminated butcher-block tops. Wood countertops must be meticulously cleaned and require periodic maintenance.

Natural Stone. Stone tends to be the most expensive countertop. Marble is relatively soft and porous and requires rigorous care in a kitchen setting. Slate and soapstone are sometimes used for countertops, but the most popular choice is granite. Durable and easy to maintain, granite may suit a country mood better in a matte rather than a polished finish. Porous stone requires sealing.

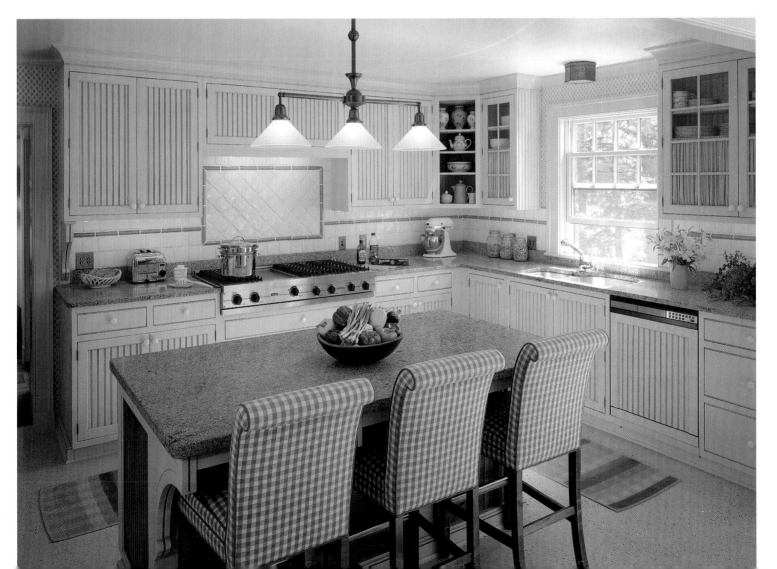

Natural stone, though expensive, fashions a classic countertop of great durability, above left.

Sealed butcher-block, above right, is another handsome natural material.

For variety of color, pattern, and texture, ceramic tile, below, is hard to beat.

Ceramic Tile. Durable, nonabsorbent glazed ceramic tile resists stains, heat, and fading, and spans the greatest range of color and pattern, from dainty florals to bold, rustic squares. But the material is unforgiving to items that are easily breakable. The grout is a weak point for tile. It's easier to maintain if the joint is tight and flush to the surface. Use a grout that's made of an impervious epoxy or a latex-modified formulation. Tiles with a rustic, handmade look may require a wider, sanded grout joint, which you should periodically seal against stains and bacteria. It's also a good idea to clean any countertop regularly with a nonabrasive antibacterial cleanser. Tile that is well maintained will last a lifetime.

Tile spans a wide price range, and the cost has to include skilled installation on a firmly reinforced backing. Countertop tiles should be specified as scratch- and acid-resistant. The countertop edge can be finished with rounded bullnose trim pieces or wood edging.

KITCHEN FLOORING

No floor takes more abuse than the kitchen's, which is subject to high traffic, dropped kitchenware, spills, grease, water, and harsh cleansers. Yet it's still expected to make a stylish contribution to the room's overall design. In any material, light-colored floors add an airy look but will require more scrupulous housekeeping. A floor that is dark tends to be less demanding, visually and logistically, but it may make a small room feel confining. You'll have to weigh your choice against how much time you have for upkeep and the actual size of the space. Whatever your circumstances, here are the most popular flooring products today.

Wood. Classic hardwood flooring and newer wood-look laminate floors evoke a country feeling in any room. For kitchen use, wood must be particularly well sealed to avoid moisture damage. Pine and fir are the less expensive options, but they aren't as durable as costlier maple, birch, oak,

and ash. Color stains or stencilied patterns may be appropriate, especially in a rustic country kitchen.

Authentic wood floors will probably take a beating in a busy kitchen. That means refinishing periodically—sanding and recoating with a tough polyurethane, for example. Laminate products are easy to keep clean, using a damp mop. But they won't hold up as long as a well-maintained real wood floor.

Eat-in corners, above, where the family takes daily meals, deserve special consideration. In this nook, framed in rugged stone and warm wood, the simple wraparound bench stands ready for extra guests.

Vinyl. For kitchens, resilient vinyl flooring is a standard choice. It's cost effective, comfortable underfoot, potentially more merciful on dropped breakables, and available in myriad designs. Though easy to maintain with a damp mop, most resilients will eventually need a liquid polish if you want a floor that shines. Vinyl products simulating wood, brick, stone, or tile aren't necessarily going to fool anyone, but they feature easy-to-live-with, dirt-hiding patterns with a pleasant country attitude. Abstract or speckled patterns can add visual texture.

Ceramic Tile. Beyond its countertop applications, ceramic tile makes a long-lasting, easy-to-keep floor with a handsome aura of authenticity and history. Like any hard floor, however, it is cold, is tiring to stand on, echoes noise, and is unkind to a dropped teacup. Some judiciously placed rugs can help overcome these disadvantages. Unglazed tiles are simply the hard-fired clay body, the same natural color throughout, from pale sand to deep umber or tinted with minerals.

The more highly fired the product, the denser, harder, and less absorbent it becomes. Low-fired earthenware terra-cotta tiles are rugged and rustic but porous. They require frequent sealing and extra maintenance in a kitchen setting. Higher-fired stoneware quarry tiles still provide a handsome, earthy look and bear up to heavy use if well sealed. Most highly fired and more expensive tiles are smooth, impervious porcelain pavers, which require no sealing.

To enliven unglazed tiles without losing their neutral earthiness, lay them in intriguing overall patterns, such as octagons, squares, herringbones, or basket weaves. Standard floor mosaics, usually with porcelain bodies, can be factory mounted on mesh sheets in custom patterns. Plain mosaics have a charming retro flair.

Glazed tiles, permanently sealed with a thin, impervious glasslike layer, open up even more decorative possibilities. Tile industry organizations test and rate glazes for durability, so make sure your choice is specified for a demanding floor application, particularly if the kitchen has an exterior entrance.

FINISHING TOUCHES

After assembling the kitchen's working parts, add the flourishes that make the whole less workaday. Paint is often the cheapest form of embellishment. Wainscoting, applied with precut tongue-and-groove planks or scored panels, can effectively dress walls, too. Of course, wallpaper is the easiest way to add pattern and print to your kitchen. You can choose from florals, checks, plaids, ticking stripes, or themed motifs, or look for designs that reinforce your country decorating style. Many manufacturers carry different lines that might include American, English, French, Italian, or Swedish country style, as well as Victorian, Shaker, and Arts and Crafts motifs, among others. Some wallpapers can be authentic reproductions, too.

Fabric softens the severity of a working kitchen, so bring on an assortment of harmonious patterns—lively chintzes, small-scale calico prints, classic checks, and stripes—for café curtains or simple shades, tablecloths, and chair pads. Picking up a fabric motif for a stenciled border can link the various elements.

Most kitchens can make room for a few carefully selected evocative accessories: hooked and rag rugs; a rocking chair; an ironwork or cut-tin chandelier; or a decoratively painted chest of drawers to cite just a few ideas. ✤

Forgoing standard wall cabinets, above, gives this room an open, unfitted look.

Hanging racks, opposite top, can instantly create a friendly display of collected kitchenware.

Finishing touches such as a checkerboard painted floor, colorful plates, and loose, light curtains, opposite bottom, soften the impact of this kitchen's heavy-duty equipment.

10

A COUNTRY BATH
With Efficient Style

lthough the ancient Greeks and Romans, along with other prosperous early civilizations, maintained luxurious public bathhouses, it was a long road to the private, plumbed-in tub with the toilet alongside that we know today. A relatively modern convenience, the bathroom typically packs lots of essential equipment into a small space, so it's in special need of old-fashioned details to become part of a welcoming country house.

In the 1790s the French produced shoe-shaped bathtubs; Benjamin Franklin brought one back to the United States so he could enjoy soaking, reading, and relaxing for hours.

But before the late nineteenth century, for most Americans, bathing was utilitarian. Periodically, someone filled a portable tub with hand-pumped and stove-heated water from buckets, and each family member had a turn.

By the 1870s the houses of well-to-do Americans had flush toilets, but only the wealthiest owned a plumbed-in tub in the same room. Most folks endured the inconvenience of chamber pots, water pitchers, and washbowls in their bedrooms. Finally, nearing the twentieth century, plumbing became increasingly common, and average homeowners carved out bathroom space from a bedroom. The old-fashioned claw-foot tub not only resembled formal furniture pieces but kept the often unreliable plumbing more accessible. Into the 1920s and '30s, closed-in tubs and crisp white tile became fashionable, celebrating thoroughly modern convenience.

TODAY'S TYPICAL BATHROOM

Though the recent trend has been toward larger bathrooms, the standard is still focused on efficient use of space. This offers the decorator an unexpected side benefit, because even minor flourishes and ornamentation go a long way toward making the bathroom attractive and full of character. Follow these simple steps to make this sometimes sterile room charming in a country-style way.

smart steps **one** **Design it to suit its use.** Not only are we spoiled with indoor plumbing, we have come to expect more than one bathroom. With bathrooms in such abundance, each may be slanted toward a different role, with different decorating demands and possibilities.

The master bath is a private retreat, deserving some luxurious amenities, such as a makeup table, TV and sound system, exercise equipment, or spa features. Space permitting, it can hold a piece or two of country furniture, such as a painted bench, an armoire, a wicker chair, or an added cabinet.

A family bathroom, on the other hand, may be where everyone showers or bathes—even the dog. It requires ample storage for toys, towels, and toiletries for kids and grownups. So keep an eye out for big baskets, quaint containers, shelves, and a capacious hamper for laundry. Because space is at often a premium, seek out useful shelves, towel bars, magazine racks, storage containers, and robe hooks styled with a bit of panache, whether in ceramic, brass, hand-painted finishes, or unusual materials. Everything should be water resistant and easy to clean, too.

Powder rooms are half-baths often located in the house's social or "public" areas. Because they're not subject to long, steamy showers or much of the morning get-up-and-go routine, durability and storage are less of an issue. Here you can indulge your decorating with delicate, eye-catching finishes, pretty collections, or displays that enhance the space.

two **Apply general decorating principles.** Even if it's a small space, assess the room's strengths and weaknesses. A room's odd angles and small size can seem picturesque in lively, high-contrast finishes. Think about harmonies of scale, proportion, line, and color spiced with subtle differences. Because a bathroom tends toward slick modern surfaces, rough baskets and earthenware pots of ferns might be refreshing. Light finishes visually enlarge a small space, but wall-to-wall pastels can seem dull without a few bright notes.

A candle flame and fresh sunflowers, opposite, beautifully accent the golden hues of this formal area. The classic crossbar faucet and marble vanity complement the antiqued cabinet.

The soft sky blue of the dormer walls, below, and the honey-brown wood floors accentuate the naturalness of a true country-style bath.

three Borrow ideas from other rooms. Bathrooms can be too utilitarian, so have fun with unexpected elements, such as elaborate window treatments, handsome moldings, a slipper-chair, potted plants, and artwork, as long as the materials can hold up to dampness.

FIXTURES

As in the kitchen, even bathrooms designed in the most authentic country spirit can accommodate modern accoutrements. Consider a reproduction of a high-tank Victorian-style toilet, claw-foot tub, and classic gooseneck faucet with porcelain crosshandles.

Antique fixtures may be an attractive addition to your bathroom, but the inconvenience of future repairs may be a drawback.

TOILETS

Many country decorators choose standard, unobtrusive wares, often in versatile white or neutral, and concentrate their decorating efforts on elements and accessories that are easy to change, such as paint, wallpaper, linens, and rugs.

Basic two-piece toilets in white vitreous china are unassuming features in a country scheme, though more expensive, sleek, contemporary one-piece models may be your preference. New toilets feature a variety of internal mechanisms

White tile set in a brick pattern, above, evokes a strong sense of style in this bathroom adorned with a vintage lavatory and reproduction fittings.

designed to meet a low-flush standard of using 1.6 gallons or less per flush. In addition to standard gravity-fed mechanisms, pressure-assisted systems use internal water pressure to compress air, which creates a more forceful flush.

TUBS AND SHOWERS

The tub and shower areas have the greatest visual weight in the room's design. Though they're most economical when combined (and a tub makes the most assuredly leakproof shower pan), the trend, especially in the master bath, is to separate the functions by creating separate fixtures for them. Tubs and shower enclosures can be found in a wide range of materials and styles. Cast-iron tubs are an attractive addition to any bathroom. However, the easier installation and lighter weight of modern plastics and ceramics make them more practical.

To keep the water contained, a clear glass shower door will do the job. A shower curtain, particularly if it consists of a waterproof liner combined with a frivolous fabric drapery, can add a soft, colorful, and easy-to-change touch amid all the hard surfaces. You can also pull it almost completely out of the way to show off any decorative tilework or handsome fittings within the tub alcove.

An antique apothecary sign, below, caps off a collection of items that merge to create a decorative yet functional personal space.

SINKS AND FITTINGS

Bathroom sinks, which designers refer to as lavatories, can be made of vitreous china, cast iron, enameled steel, fiberglass, solid-surfacing material, stone, faux stone, or metal. Pedestal sinks or wall-mounted lavatories with metal or carved-wood legs encompass a variety of handsome vintage styles. Remember, today a beautiful fixture can stand alone as a piece of sculpture in the room.

Faucets. Faucets span a wide price range. In appearance, they can be considered as "jewelry" for the bathroom when fabricated in rich vintage styles, perhaps with china or bright crosshandles and a gooseneck spout. Brass is the traditional finish, but chrome can look at home fashioned after nostalgic styles. Single-lever controls, though undeniably modern, are convenient and easy to use.

VANITIES

The vanity is often the keynote of a bathroom's country style because cabinet-making is a venerable craft. An old but not valuable cabinet, small chest of

SMART TIP

SAFETY

In this room where accidents can easily happen, decorating choices should bow to safety. Here are a few pointers:

Floors and bathtub floors should be slip resistant.

Rugs should have antiskid backing.

Be wary of glass collectibles and hard surfaces.

For the sake of sleepy people in semidarkness, avoid changes in floor level.

Install antiscald fixtures and ground-fault circuit interrupters (GFCIs) at the electrical outlets.

drawers, or table can be converted into a charming vanity, though it must be carefully sealed against water. You'll also find vanities with evocative country details made of rustic pine, smooth maple, or pickled oak, with planked or raised panel doors. Stock cabinetry often works well in standardized bathroom spaces. Custom cabinetry opens up more options and may offer accessories such as matching display shelves, moldings, or a bracket for a vase or candle.

FINISHING TOUCHES

Bathrooms use many of the same practical finishing materials as kitchens. Wood instantly adds warmth and character and a "furnished" feeling. In the bath, consider softwoods such as fir, redwood, and pine or dense hardwoods like teak and maple for tongue-and-groove wainscoting, moldings, or furniture pieces.

Mirrors enhance a sense of space, albeit with a harder modern look. Downplay this by extending the mirror into a corner or framing it with molding.

Ceramic tile is a classic bathroom material, and it can be the decorative stand-out. There are some options to lend interest to a low-key background—for example, a play of different shapes, such as triangles, squares, and rectangles interlocked on a white wall. Or turn the square grid diagonally for an energetic diamond design. Try a stamped high-relief pattern or a heavy rope-molding trim to give a plain color more tactile appeal. Clay-colored tones and faux stone add a natural spirit to bare white walls and floors.

LIGHTING

In a room where people shave, put on makeup, remove splinters, and the like, good lighting, both natural and artificial, is essential.

Just as in any room, windows add light and charm to a bath. Those with divided-light sashes or projected bays add particular elegance. Skylights and clerestory windows can fetch sunlight with no worries about privacy.

All bathroom lighting fixtures should be suitable for damp areas. A ceiling-mounted fixture, perhaps a bowl-type pendant or a smaller chandelier, can cast a good general glow. Paired wall sconces alongside the mirror eliminate the shadows that can be cast by an overhead source.

ACCESSORIES

In limited space, every added object should be carefully chosen. Some fanciful touches with a country sensibility might include a vintage sugar and creamer set to hold toothbrushes and cottonballs. An old teapot can be a charming planter or a place to store combs and brushes.

And don't forget the old model-home trick of displaying big fluffy towels to instantly make the room feel cozy and welcoming. 🍐

A classic white wooden slat wall, opposite, provides the perfect backdrop to display a multihued glass assortment.

Earth colors and an antiqued mirror establish a country feeling in this modern-day bath, below.

GLOSSARY

Analogous Color Scheme: A combination focused on neighboring hues on the color wheel. The shared underlying color generally gives such schemes a coherent flow.

Antiquing: Any technique used to make a surface look old; usually refers to a thin glaze that is applied to a surface, allowing the undercoat to show through.

Arts and Crafts Style: A design movement that began in England during the late nineteenth century and became popular in America during the early twentieth century. Led by William Morris, the movement rejected industrialization and encouraged fine craftsmanship and design simplicity.

Bobbin Lace: A lace woven with long threads, weighted with hanging bobbins, and then pinned over a patterned pillow. Also called pillow lace.

Builder Style: A term used to designate many houses built between 1895 and 1930 that do not adhere to a particular style; generally divided into four categories: homestead, foursquare, bungalow, and cottage.

Bungalow Style: A category of the Builder Style that features low dormered roofs, front porches, and the use of natural materials.

Carpenter Gothic: A version of Gothic Revival–style architecture rendered in wood to create cottages and farmhouses characterized by steep gables, straight lines, intricate scrollwork, and gingerbread trim.

Chintz: A cotton fabric, often in a floral print, that is coated with a resin to give it sheen.

Colonial Style: An early American architectural and decorative style of the Colonial period that was influenced by design ideas brought by settlers from Europe, particularly England. This basic and functional style initially featured a minimum of ornament but became more elaborate with the prosperity of the Colonies.

Color-Washing: A paint technique that consists of random layers of thin glaze that are blended to produce a faded, uneven look similar to that of whitewash.

Combing: A paint technique that involves dragging a plastic or metal comb through wet paint or glaze to simulate texture or to create a pattern.

Damask: A Jacquard-weave material made of cotton, silk, wool, or a combination with a satin, raised design. Widely used for draperies.

Distressed Finish: A surface finish that suggests age. It is produced by sanding and battering the final coat of paint or stain.

Dormer: A vertical window set into a sloping roof, or a roof that contains such a window.

Dragging: Any paint technique that involves marking narrow lines of color on a surface. Also called *strié* or combing. Dragging techniques that specifically intend to imitate wood are called woodgraining techniques.

Federal Style: An architectural and decorative style popular in America during the early nineteenth century featuring symmetrical rooms and classical ornamentation.

Gothic Revival Style: An architectural and decorative style popular in America during the mid-nineteenth century that romanticized the design forms of the medieval period, including elements such as pointed arches and trefoils (three-leaf motifs).

Georgian Style: An English architectural and decorative style popular during the late eighteenth century, with rooms characterized by the systematic use of paneling, other classically inspired woodwork, and bold colors.

Greek Revival Style: An architectural and decorative style of the nineteenth century that drew inspiration from ancient Greek designs. Its dignified motifs include the Greek key and acanthus and classical elements, such as pediments and columns.

Jacquard Loom: A loom named after its inventor, which revolutionized weaving by using punched cards to produce intricate designs.

Majolica: A type of glazed earthenware decorated in lively colors, from the nineteenth century.

Marbling: A decorative paint technique that uses specific tools, paint, and glaze to create the appearance of marble.

Mochaware: Earthenware from the nineteenth century that is decorated with swirls made from drips of colored acid on wet slip.

Neoclassical Style: Any revival of the ancient styles of Greece and Rome, particularly during the late eighteenth and early nineteenth centuries. The shapes and ornaments of ancient architecture were also applied to furniture design.

Pilgrim Furniture: A style of furniture that has medieval aspects, featuring straight legs and banister-like backs with lathe-made turnings.

Queen Anne Style: An architectural style that was popular in America between 1870 and 1910 as a variation on the Victorian home, with gingerbread trim, gables, dormers, chimneys, and porches.

Scherenshnitte: An intricate design made from paper, used in German folk art.

Scrimshaw: A carved piece of ivory or the act of producing scrimshaw.

Shaker Style: A furniture style introduced by the Shakers, a religious sect that valued the plain and practical and used a minimum of ornament.

Shingle Style: An architectural style that uses textured shingles painted in red, gray, brown, olive green, or yellow to cover the exterior; particularly popular in coastal areas in the Northeast.

Spattering: The paint technique of applying random dots of paint over a surface by striking a saturated brush or rubbing paint through a screen.

Stippling: A paint technique that involves pouncing a special brush straight up and down over a surface, creating myriad tiny dots that blend together when viewed from a distance.

Terra-Cotta Tile: Molded nonvitreous or semivitreous unglazed tiles, often of a reddish color.

Tole: A painted household metal used from the eighteenth century onward for trays, lamp shades, and other ornamental wares.

Tramp Art: A style of wood carving prevalent from 1875 to 1930, usually used to decorate small crafts.

Trompe L'Oeil: French for "fool the eye"—used to describe a painted surface that convincingly mimics reality.

Valance: A short curtain that hangs along the top part of a window, with or without a curtain underneath. It can also be made of wood or metal that is painted or covered with fabric.

Veneer: A thin sheet of high-quality wood used as a surface material.

Wainscoting: Traditionally, paneling or woodwork that covers the lower third of a wall.

RESOURCES

THE AMERICAN ARCHITECTURAL FOUNDATION
1735 New York Ave. NW
Washington, DC 20006
Phone: 202-626-7500
Fax: 202-626-7420
www.amerarchfoundation.com
The American Architectural Foundation is a nonprofit organization that educates people about the importance of architecture.

**THE AMERICAN INSTITUTE FOR
CONSERVATION OF HISTORIC AND
ARTISTIC WORKS**
1717 K St. NW, Ste. 200
Washington, DC 20006
Phone: 202-452-9545
Fax: 202-452-9328
Info@aic-faic.org
www.aic.stanford.edu
This institution focuses on preserving art and historic artifacts for cultural heritage purposes. It offers helpful information on the Web site, such as how to care for your treasures or become a conservator, and links to other preservation societies.

ANTIQUE HOTSPOTS
www.antiquehotspots.com
A helpful Web site that offers information on where to find antiques on the Internet and in your area.

THE FURNITURE SOCIETY
P.O. Box 18
Free Union, VA 22940
Phone: 804-973-1488
Fax: 804-973-0336
www.furnituresociety.org
This nonprofit organization advances the art of making furniture. It fosters creativity among and promotes the education of furniture artists.

MONROE SALT WORKS
76 Bartlett Hill Rd.
Monroe, ME 04951
888-525-4471
www.monroesaltworks.com
A salt glaze stoneware company from Maine that produces pottery, furniture, and other items.

NATIONAL PAINT & COATINGS ASSOCIATION
1500 Rhode Island Ave. NW
Washington, DC 20005
Phone: 202-462-6272
Fax: 202-462-8549
www.paint.org
This nonprofit organization represents over 400 paint and coatings manufacturers.

NATIONAL TRUST FOR HISTORIC PRESERVATION
1785 Massachusetts Ave. NW
Washington, DC 20036
Phone: 202-588-6000
Fax: 202-588-6038
www.nthp.org
This organization works to protect the most endangered historical places from being developed. The Web site offers the latest news in the maintenance of these historical sites and information on becoming a member.

SHAKER WORKSHOPS
P.O. Box 8001
Ashburnam, MA 01430-8001
Phone: 800-840-9121
Fax: 978-827-6554
www.shakerworkshops.com
Shaker Workshops manufactures fine reproductions of Shaker furniture and accessories offered as DIY kits or custom-finished.

CREDITS

INDEX

INDEX

Have a home decorating, improvement, or gardening project? Look for these and other fine **Creative Homeowner books** wherever books are sold.

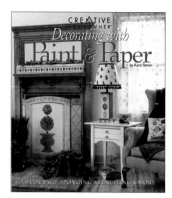

Projects to personalize your rooms with paint and paper. 300 color photos. 176 pp.; 9"×10"
BOOK #: 279723

Learn how to make the most of color. More than 150 color photos. 176 pp.; 9"×10"
BOOK #: 287264

How to create kitchen style like a pro. Over 150 color photographs. 176 pp.; 9"×10"
BOOK #: 279935

How to work with space, color, pattern, texture. Over 300 photos. 256 pp.; 9"×10"
BOOK #: 279667

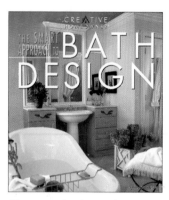

All you need to know about designing a bath. Over 150 color photos. 176 pp., 9"×10"
BOOK # 287225

Design advice and industry tips for choosing window treatments. Over 225 illustrations. 176 pp., 9"×10"
BOOK # 279431

Master stenciling, sponging, glazing, marbling, and more. Over 300 illustrations. 272 pp., 9"×10"
BOOK #: 279550

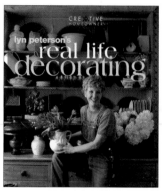

Interior designer Lyn Peterson's easy-to-live-with decorating ideas. Over 350 photos. 304 pp., 9"×10"
BOOK #: 279382

Impressive guide to garden design and plant selection. More than 600 color photos. 320 pp.; 9"×10"
BOOK #: 274615

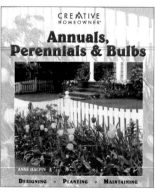

Lavishly illustrated with portraits of over 100 flowering plants; more than 500 photos. 208 pp.; 9"×10"
BOOK #: 274032

How to design and build a beautiful deck. Over 500 color photos and illustrations. 192 pp.; 8½"×10⅞"
BOOK #: 277162

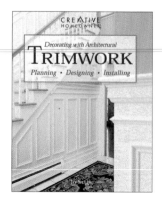

How to create a richly textured home. 360 color photos and illustrations. 208 pp; 8½" ×10⅞"
BOOK #: 277495